Endorsements

Out of the Ashes is riveting and very well written. We have worked in this field for over twenty years and have rarely found a family that discovered and then went through the healing process together. Counselors, pastors, caregivers, and prayer ministers will find this book extremely helpful and encouraging. Survivors will find validation and hope as they read how God intervenes and brings healing to families. This book is a tribute to courage in the face of deep grief.

—**Cheryl Knight**, MTh and **Jo Getzinger**, MSW
Founders of C.A.R.E., Inc.

Throughout my thirty-nine years of pastoral experiences, I have read and studied hundreds of books for both professional study and pleasure, yet I have found this book, *Out of the Ashes,* to be one of the most jolting, shocking, and disturbing accounts of a family facing spiritual warfare. It is a book of personal and parental betrayal, but it is also a portrait of the benefits of having a loving heavenly Father ... a story of the total depravity of man and the thorough deliverance of God ... a narrative of a family's journey out of the ashes and into restoration through the promises of God. *Out of the Ashes* is a must-read of real hope and change, a celebration of God's faithfulness and healing.

—**Pastor Larry D. Connors**
Masters of Divinity, Grace Theological Seminary
Pastor for thirty-nine years

OUT OF THE ASHES

OUT OF THE ASHES

A FORGED FAITH JOURNEY IN CONFRONTING AND OVERCOMING EVIL

HANNAH S. BROWN

WinePressPublishing
Great Books, Defined.

WinePress Publishing (PO Box 428, Enumclaw, WA 98022) functions only as book publisher. As such, the ultimate design, content, editorial accuracy, and views expressed or implied in this work are those of the author.

ISBN 13: 978-1-4141-2295-3
ISBN 10: 1-4141-2295-0
Library of Congress Catalog Card Number: 2012900291

This book is dedicated to the Father, the Son, and the Holy Spirit. It is His story, and we are His family. If all of mankind and creation were to praise Him for all of eternity, with all of their beings, there would still remain a void, lacking the worship He is due. Here, my beloved, Papa, this is for you. Be glorified and eternally praised. I love you.

Your girl forever,
Hannah

CONTENTS

FOREWORD

WE MET HANNAH Brown for the first time in a small local coffee shop, shortly after Holly's birth. We had mutual friends who were visiting us from out of the area, so for the sake of convenience, we all gathered at the bistro. We were quickly drawn to the warmth of this family. Their commitment and love for each other and for the Lord captured our hearts. It was refreshing to find such a close-knit family that talked the talk and walked the walk.

When given the news of their "suddenly," we recoiled in shock and disbelief. Up to this point in our lives, we had not experienced such horrific evil related to someone so close to our hearts. Rather than withdraw from feeling inadequate in the situation, we pressed closer.

While listening with tears in our eyes as painful discoveries were related, we would offer small comforts—a freshly brewed cup of tea, a caress for a small face full of fear, or a favorite lullaby hummed while embracing. When your normal life has been shattered, and you are forced to cope with a new normal, the mundane and routine responsibilities of life can provide a brief means of escape.

Out of the Ashes is the story of this family's journey from betrayal, abuse, and devastation to one of healing, restoration, and hope. Our Lord can redeem the broken and shattered places of our lives and make them whole again.

As in most cases, the journey of life is not a straight path, but one that takes us down many different avenues. In reading this true story, you will find encouragement, hope, and strength to face your own "suddenlies."

It has been our privilege to walk beside this family and be a part of their journey. Our hearts and lives have been forever touched and changed.

—Reverend Don and **Kathy Ballantyne**
Sozo Ministry, Pacific Northwest

The following account is true, and the names have been changed for privacy. The reference to Child Protection Services is a pseudonym for a similar branch that coordinates with this organization. General areas are intentionally given rather than actual states or counties. References to materials, publications, or ministries are not their endorsement of the beliefs or views of this account. They are simply resources that the author used as part of the recovery process. This account and its views are those of the author in the realm of personal experience and not from a professional or licensed position.

He crouches, he lies low, that the helpless may
fall by his strength. He has said in his heart, "God has
forgotten; He hides His face; He will never see."

—Psalm 10:10–11

CHAPTER 1

"SUDDENLIES"

THERE ARE "SUDDENLIES" in life that reaffirm the fallacy of human control. The moment the suddenly occurs, it becomes the pivotal point where everything shifts. No one sees a suddenly coming; it is not something you can prepare for or avoid.

People are not the same after a suddenly. They see things differently, and everything about them feels the change. Some suddenlies can be good. Ours didn't seem that way. Ours felt like a fire that intensified, leaving ashes for remains. Ashes represented loss and the scourge that singed the history of a childhood. Ashes later symbolized purification and the cleansing of land. Ashes were required for cleansing the temple in Jerusalem after it had been defiled (Numbers 19). Ashes were where Job sat and remained faithful in the midst of his loss. The "suddenly" led to the ashes, which led to being wrapped in a glory that exchanged ashes for beauty and praise.

I was gazing out the upstairs window when the suddenly emerged. It was a fall afternoon in November. Fiery colors of dwarf maples edged the fence line below. The sky was a brilliant blue after days of coastal rain. I had a deep sense of joy over all the blessings God had lavished on our family. Our new home (filled with our beautiful children) was like a haven atop a hill. Anticipating the coming holidays, I was mentally planning ways to make them more meaningful and less chaotic. I turned from the window when my daughter Ann came in with the phone.

"Mom, it's Aunt Ellen. She sounds upset."

Ellen, with panic in her voice, recounted what my seven-year-old niece, Diana, had shared about her recent sleepover at Grandpa's. I had her repeat herself, stopping her for clarity. Everything in my mind sharply narrowed its focus, trying to grasp what she was saying. Her words were blows to my chest, and I struggled to catch my breath as she continued.

"Do you remember if your dad did anything like this to you when you were little? Do you?"

"No, Ellen, not that I remember. Maybe she got the wrong face mixed with the event. She could have seen something on TV and is confused. It could've been someone who looked like him, and he reminded her of something that had happened."

"I just don't know what to think. What should I do?"

"It will be okay, Ellen. Let's first try to find out how sure she is; we don't know yet. I'll call our pastor and Nick and find out what we should do. I'll call you back tonight."

I slumped to the floor, shaking. Grabbing the side of the bed to pull myself up, I prayed. "Oh, God, please help me! Please, please help me!"

Quickly, I dialed my husband, Nick. There was no answer. Then I called my friend Becky, who lived nearby.

"I'll come over and stay with you until Nick comes home. You need someone with you. I'll be there in fifteen minutes."

My mind scoured through a catalogue of memories, searching for any awareness that would help me make sense of my conversation with Ellen. I thought about the struggle I had over the spiritual veneer my parents seemed to wear. There was a dryness you could feel when you were around them but could not see in their daily lives. There were rational reasons to try and excuse it: they were older now, they were gone a lot on RV trips and away from church, and they held some different doctrinal views than I did.

Inside of me an inner dialogue of conflicting thoughts debated opposing views. This was contrary to all I knew about my father. I had grown up respecting, admiring, and honoring him. Who wouldn't? Dad had dug the trenches for the footings of the Christian school I attended. I handed him the nails when he framed its walls. He had been a deacon and school board member, served on the city council and the zoning board, been a respected businessman and an avid supporter of missions … and the list went on.

Diana had to be mistaken! My brother and sister-in-law lived in a mess of a house with minimal supervision of their children. That's why my parents watched their kids so often. Travis's depression and constant unemployment and Ellen's bad health and mood swings gave the children too much time in the care of others. Perhaps it was their neighbor; I had tried to tell Ellen not to send her kids over there. The lady lived with an unstable boyfriend we suspected had a drinking problem. And then the shows the kids watched on the television—well the odds that Diana had seen something she shouldn't have was a given.

But good men can fall, right? If he had been in a state of spiritual dryness, then he was vulnerable. Even so, something like this did not make sense—unless he had a pornography addiction that had progressed and now involved a perverted fixation on little girls. If he did, maybe the struggle had been caught early enough that nothing worse had happened. He just needed some help, and then everything would be okay.

But then, why would Diana say what she did? A little child didn't make this stuff up unless she had been exposed or something bad had really happened. What if she was right? What if he had done this, and if so, what about our girls and the times he had been with them? No, I never left them alone in his care like Travis had done with his daughters. I always left them with Mom. Dad was lousy on picking out age-appropriate movies, and I didn't trust him to discipline any of our children. He had been too harsh with my brothers when they were younger. Of course, that was thirty years ago, and he seemed to have mellowed a lot, but still … Mom knew the rules: no spanking and only movies I approved. Mom always assured me that she'd make sure my instructions for the children were followed, especially with the younger ones.

Before Nick got home from work, I called our district pastor. He listened and prayed with me, and then he asked if I would be reporting the abuse or if my brother Travis would. If we didn't report, he would because he was a state-mandated reporter. Someone would have to report, and we needed to have Diana checked out as part of that process.

Nick and I called Travis and Ellen that night after Becky left. We told them that our pastor said they would have to take Diana to the Child's Protection Service (CPS) for filing a report and evaluation. Travis said he needed the rest of the week to think (we gave him the weekend), until we returned from the coast. My folks had given us one of their weekends at their timeshare as an early anniversary present. We decided to go this weekend, while we could. Who knew how things would be with them when we returned? Our eldest son, Joseph, said he would watch his younger siblings and arranged things with his work schedule so we could go. I was nursing our newborn daughter, Phoebe, so she came along.

The ocean waves were calming to my soul. Nick and I sat quietly, taking in the beauty of the Atlantic coast, but the moments of shared silence were broken by an undertow of nagging questions. "Could this be true? How could this be real?" We had an uneasy sense that we would be walking a difficult path in the days ahead—one we had never walked before, nor ever thought we would. Why would we? After all, Nick and I had come from good families with strong Christian values and beliefs.

As we drove home along the coast, I savored the cool breeze, the cloudless sky contrasted against the backdrop of the forest, and the jagged rocks strewn along the sandy shore. It was a beautiful day. We stopped and purchased fudge for the children at a local candy store, snapped silly pictures, changed Phoebe, and headed home with our windows down. I wanted all of this about my dad to have been a mistake, a false accusation, someone else. I wanted the ocean breeze, Nick's arm against mine, and Phoebe's sweet sleeping face to be all I had to think on, but it wasn't.

On Monday, Nick called Travis. Travis told him he thought that it would be best to figure this out after the holidays. He didn't want to upset things until then. Nick told him "no." We needed to know if Diana was telling the truth; our girls could have been harmed too. Even though our kids all assured us that Grandpa had not touched them in a wrong way, we still needed to know if it was safe for the kids to be around him. We needed to know if this was just the fruit of Diana's home life or reality. Nick told Travis that if he didn't call CPS, we would, and that would make Travis look like a non-protective parent. Travis swore, cursed at Nick, and hung up.

Ellen called the next day. The call had been made, and Diana was scheduled for an interview and an exam.

The CPS report came back a week later. Diana was not confused. Child Protection Services confirmed Dad was the perpetrator, and Travis's other children would also be examined. From that moment on, everything changed.

CHAPTER 2

MOM

TRAVIS WANTED ME to tell Mom. Every time he thought of calling her, he would fall apart. He was depressed, too depressed to think straight. He didn't want Mom to find out, when the cops showed up on their doorstep, that Dad had molested Diana.

I called Mom and asked if we could go out for lunch. She wondered why I hadn't included Dad in our plans. It wasn't like me. She was right.

"Just need a girl time, a woman-to-woman talk, without Dad," I said.

"Could you give me a clue as to what this is about?" she pleaded. I couldn't.

"Just need to talk, Mom, I will tell you at lunch."

Dad's and my relationship had changed in the last two years. We had not been close for a long time. I felt belittled and criticized by Dad when I was young and afraid of him too. He had been harsh and stern, and I had quickly learned to be a good little girl to keep him happy. One would have called me the "good sheep of the family," I suppose. In school, the kids made fun of me. I was "little Miss Goodie Two Shoes," "Miss Holier Than Thou," and "teacher's pet." In spite of the ridicule, I still worked hard to please Daddy. In my teen years, I seemed to push myself, continually hoping to finally get that "well done" from him, but it never came. As an adult, I finally realized I would never meet his standards, as each time I thought I had, the bar moved. I realized too that I didn't have to please Dad; God liked me for *me*.

After a visit with my dad that had ended with him being crabby and critical, I drove away hurt. I told the Lord in my frustration, "If I had to choose him for a friend, I wouldn't, but because he's my father, I'm stuck with him! At least I stand to inherit a lot of money!"

Then I felt convicted and told God from my heart that in truth I would gladly trade his money for a good relationship with him.

The Lord's response was strong and quickly redirected my thoughts: *"How long will you value his words said about you and spoken over you above Mine? Don't I merit your allegiance above his? Who is your daddy really?"*

From that day on, I was no longer the same. My earthly father's words stopped hurting the way they had. I felt separated from them, as though they fell to the ground, never reaching my heart. I had worked through pain, anger, and forgiveness, and I had aligned my heart with my real Daddy, my Abba-Father.

Over time, though, my dad did seem to change; he was kinder and less critical. He had retired and was no longer under the pressures of work. He had mellowed and enjoyed playing with our children. We had lived on opposite shores of the country for several years. Nick's work had brought us to the West Coast, and the distance apart had been good for Dad and me. Now Nick's employer needed his expertise at the East Coast facility so we moved and were living closer to my parents. Dad seemed to want to make up for the lost time and relocated from a few hours south of us to a home ten miles away. We would often go out for espresso, or he would invite me along when he and Mom went shopping in the city. He liked to discuss politics, news, end-time events, and his grandchildren with me. He would plan fun things we could all do together or offer to help with projects Nick and I were working on at the house. We would laugh and play cards together, and it felt like my little girl's dream of having my daddy like me had come true.

Then at Christmas, he would go all out, and I would scold him, "It is too much!"

His eyes would soften when I hugged and thanked him. "Love you too," he would say.

Mom would remind me of how they never had much when I was little, and Dad had missed out on being able to give. He had missed out on enjoying his children when we were small, having to work so hard just to get by. It made him happy to be able to give to us now. I would stack on shelves or stuff in closets the opulence they bestowed upon the children, and the heirlooms and gifts they lavished on Nick and me.

The day Mom and I were to meet for lunch, Joseph offered to come along. He felt protective of me. From the quiet, tearful discussions with Nick, and the questions we had asked him and the other children about their grandfather, he knew something was amiss. I told him what we knew so far. He offered to drive and planned to sit in the parking lot and pray for me while I talked with my mom.

Before I got out of the car, he leaned over and hugged me. "You'll do fine, Mom."

I walked into the cafe with no thought of food. I would just get a Coke to settle my stomach, or a coffee. Mom was already there, waiting. I slid into the booth across from her. She reached out and took my hand.

"What's up, Honey? Talk to me."

I told her that Diana said a man had … and I described the whole disgusting thing. Mom's mouth dropped open.

"Well, do they know who did this?" she asked.

"Yes."

"Are they sure?"

"Yes, Mom, she was examined by CPS, and CPS confirmed that Diana told them the truth. She knows for sure who did it."

"Well, who, who did this?"

"Mom, Dad did."

"What, who?"

"Dad. Dad did."

"How could this be? He doesn't fit the profile of a pedophile!"

Mom had served in the House of Representatives; she had been a politician who had enacted tough laws against men like the one now being accused. She had researched the behavior of pedophiles in her effort to form these laws; and the General Assembly, the County Commission

8

on Obscenity and Pornography, and the County Board of Supervisors had honored her for her accomplishments.

The rest of the conversation was Mom going from denial to: "He better not have hurt my babies!"

I gave her the names of some good counselors that I had found and the number for a place that helped men with struggles like Dad's. I told her I would be calling her brother Dwight. I didn't want her to go through this alone. I would be limited in how much I could be there for her at this time, at least until we knew more. She seemed relieved that I would tell her brother.

I informed her that the police would be paying them a visit soon, that we were still in the process of determining if any of the other girls had been harmed, and that the holidays together were off. Then I stated that if Dad had hurt my children, I would have to forgive him. Little did I know how profound, prophetic, and challenging those words would be in the days ahead. She ended our talk. She needed to go tell Dad. I cautioned her to make sure she put the guns away first, as Dad could become irrational or severely depressed. I told her not to support any of his denial but to help him get help.

"I am not going to hug you. I don't want to cry." She stood abruptly, straightened her blouse, and left.

I waited until she was gone, and then I got the tab. Neither of us had ordered lunch. I had a bad feeling that this was the last time we would be together, and there was no hug good-bye.

Mom had been her stoic self: the one who had a plastic shell and didn't cry, the one who seemed like a puppet to me—disconnected, impersonal, and controlled. The one I had seen at her mother's funeral. My grandma was always poised, like a queen, and carried herself elegantly. Mom thought being composed at her funeral was a way to honor her. She refused to cry and told me that Grandma would have been proud of her for her behavior.

There were different sides to Mom. There were times I would pick up the phone and call her, only to hear irritation in her voice. After we talked, I would tell Nick, "It was my crabby mom this time. I will have to call back a different time."

When she was like that, she seemed to forget some of our conversation, as though she was distracted and stressed. While she had not been the crabby mom during our meeting, she had worn the shell well, faking a need to keep composure.

In reality, it had been a long time since I had seen the part of my mom I called my "real mom." Sometimes when Dad was away, she would actually slow down and listen, and she seemed less distracted and more like the real mom I rarely saw. It was then that I felt closer to the real her, as though the barriers of fear and control had cracked open and she could peek out.

Two days after our lunch, the phone rang. It was the "real mom," and she sounded afraid. In hushed tones she hurriedly told me that Dad had just gone out to the car; she was taking him to a counselor. She wanted me to tell Travis to have Kristine (Travis's older daughter) checked out too. Then she told me to take care of Travis and to "keep doing what I was doing" and hung up. She acted as if she was frightened of what might happen if Dad came in and heard her talking. I felt concern for her safety.

I called back the following morning to check on her, but the real mom was gone, only the plastic mom answered the phone. I asked her about the counseling appointment. She said that until Dad had gone through the legal process, counseling would be impossible. It seemed they either had left the session midway or had not even gone. I asked her if she felt safe. Then a different side of Mom surfaced, a side I had never experienced before. It was an eerie, robotic mom that said words like an animated machine, with no feelings, even though her words were expressed with emphatic tones.

"Ab-so-lute-ly," she said, drawing each syllable out. "Ab-so-lute-ly, I feel ab-so-lute-ly safe."

CHAPTER 3

ABUSE CONFIRMED

KRISTINE'S REPORT FROM CPS came back with confirmed abuse as well. The worst had happened, it had happened to her, and it had happened repeatedly. Charges would be filed on behalf of both of Travis's girls. Travis called to tell me that the sheriff had called him. They would be serving Dad a warrant in the next hour and had called to confirm Dad's address. I found the sheriff's alerting call to Travis and the need for the address perplexing. Didn't they know it, and why did they inform Travis prior to their arrival?

Travis's emotional instability and financial dependence upon my parents motivated him to promptly warn Dad. He informed Dad that if he would quickly drive to the sheriff's office and turn himself in, they would go easier on him and he could be released on bail. Dad turned himself in before the sheriff arrived, spent a few nights in jail, and posted $950,000 in bail.

I had not understood that a person doesn't suddenly develop a "struggle" with a perverted attraction to children. It happens over time, and it affects changes in the brain and in the person's basic sense of humanity. It isn't a matter of "catching it early." Usually, by the time the problem is known, a lot of damage has been done secretly to the most vulnerable: children from troubled homes, children too small to express what has happened, and children who had a relationship of trust with the perpetrator. Kristine had been all of the above and had frequently been in my parents' care, even more than Diana, her younger sister.

Sunday, during our church service, Nick and I went forward for prayer. One of our district pastors prayed with us and gave us a verse that would carry us in the days ahead. It was Isaiah 43:2: "When you pass through the waters, I will be with you; and through the rivers, they shall not overflow you. When you walk through the fire, you shall not be burned, nor shall the flame scorch you."

After church, our friends Irene and Bruce prayed with us as well, and Irene gave me the phone number of a Christian counselor her daughter was seeing.

"I think it will help for you to talk with her. She is helping a family in my daughter's church that is going through a similar situation." Then they invited Nick and me over for lunch.

We felt raw, and their home felt safe. I sank back into a corduroy recliner while Irene laid her hand on me and prayed, asking the Lord to bring truth to our situation. Instantly, I heard God tell me that this was of the occult.

"Occult?" I was perplexed.

"Occult means hidden," Irene explained.

In the future, I would understand that God not only meant *hidden* but also the very evil itself. After anointed prayers, warm coffee, and good food, we left their home with a sense of peace and strength.

CHAPTER 4

SECRETS AND
A MONSTER

THE NEXT DAY I called the counselor, Grace Worthington, who offered to help in any way she could. She was counseling another family dealing with sexual abuse perpetrated by a close relative. They were further down the road in the process of recovery. She asked if they would be willing to talk with us. They agreed, and Grace gave me Angela's number.

Angela shared their story of what had happened to their daughter Crystal. Crystal had been molested by her grandfather around the ages of two to three. She explained how her daughter would have re-occurring nightmares, would have accidents in her pants, and was extremely fearful at night. Crystal would also have screaming fits for no apparent reason. They could not figure out what was going on with her. Then one morning, Crystal came downstairs naked and said she was ready to go to Grandpa's. After that, they started to suspect that something was wrong. They began to question why she would go to her grandpa's naked, and little by little, Crystal's hidden torment unfolded.

As Angela talked about her daughter's behaviors, it was as if she were describing our daughter Holly. Holly also had reoccurring nightmares. At first, I thought they were from whatever my dad was watching on TV while my mother babysat her. I had scolded him about it and reminded Mom of our rules about television. Holly was only to watch the videos I dropped off or preschool age-appropriate cartoons. I reminded Dad that some cartoons were inappropriate. Rational thinking doesn't develop in children until age six or seven, and telling her it was "just pretend" didn't make sense to her.

My mom had watched Holly each Monday since she was a toddler while I taught a class at the homeschool co-op our older children attended. Mom had even taught a class to help out prior to when Holly was weaned. Then, when Holly was weaned, she offered to watch her so I could teach. She told me how much she enjoyed reading stories to Holly and taking her on little walks along the river behind their house. They would quietly watch for the occasional appearance of a Glossy Ibis or collect smooth stones. Afterwards, she would fix Holly a snack, and Holly would often fall asleep until I returned. I was usually gone two hours.

Holly was at that age where she would sometimes fuss and cling to me when I would go to leave, but she could be easily distracted. I would listen outside the front door until she stopped crying (she always stopped shortly after I closed it), just to make sure she was all right before I drove away.

Holly's clinginess had increased in the past few months. I had attributed this and her recent messy pants as a response to the last stages of my pregnancy and the arrival of her baby sister. I figured she was reverting to infant-like behavior, which some children do when they realized they will no longer be the baby of the family. Just prior to and following Phoebe's birth, she continually wanted to sleep near me, coming into my room each night with a bad dream, feeling scared, and wanting Mommy. I could only figure the tantrums she would throw were delayed two-year-old tantrums now taking place at the age of four. Holly's behavior sounded unsettlingly like Crystal's.

Oh Lord, what if something happened to her and this behavior was not what I thought?

Angela also shared how her father-in-law had threatened her daughter to keep quiet. He told her not to talk about what he was doing and that if she did, bad things would happen to her mommy. Angela explained how easy it is for someone to intimidate and confuse a child in one area so the child doesn't talk. At the same time, that person will be warm toward the child and indulge him or her in other ways. The confusion can cause a child to feel shame and believe that he or she caused the bad things to happen. Children self-blame and compartmentalize events so that they are able to embrace and behave normally with the very person who is also harming them. They don't know who the victim is and who the perpetrator is or what is wrong about the abuser's behavior. They only know they feel bad and think that they themselves are bad.

She further told me that she felt her mother-in-law had been involved in her daughter's abuse—or at least aware of it. I no longer felt confident that Holly had been protected simply because she was in my mother's care; nor was I reassured because she appeared to enjoy being with them. She would run excitedly to the door to greet them whenever she and Dad would visit our house.

I decided to question Holly in the same way Angela had talked of questioning her daughter. I would use the same words Angela said her stepfather had used with Crystal, when he told her "not to talk."

I cuddled Holly in the rocking chair and questioned her in a calm, unemotional tone. "Holly, has Grandpa ever asked you 'not to talk' about something?"

She looked down sheepishly. "Yes. Not to talk about sitting on his lap."

Holly had often sat on Grandpa's lap in our presence, so why was it a secret? Unless there were times when sitting on his lap was different than when we were there.

No, Lord, please, not our little Holly.

Several days later, Travis called. "I just had the strangest call from Dad. I think it was some kind of apology or something. He told me that Diana said that she was itchy in her private area and that he scratched her and realizes that he didn't used the best judgment there. Then he said he was just so used to scratching their backs and all that he overstepped. He told me he was sorry. I pushed the record button on my answering machine and captured part of the call on tape. He has a ___ of a lot more to confess than that!" Travis vented for a while and then hung up.

The word "scratched" caught my attention. Holly had been itching herself a lot, and I was getting frustrated at her fixation. I had changed bath soaps and used anti-yeast cream, but she still seemed too touchy in that area, and it was a puzzle to me.

15

After Travis's call, I turned to find Holly standing in the kitchen itching. Using the same word that my father had used with Travis, I asked, "Holly, why are you scratching?"

"Because it hurts." She started to cry.

"Honey, who scratched you?"

"The monster did!" she yelled abruptly.

I picked her up and held her. "What does the monster look like?"

"Like Grandpa … I think, like Grandpa."

"Scratched" had been the deceptive term my father had used; now it was the term that brought exposure. Then later that evening, Holly further informed me, "Mommy, Grandpa has a scary part and a nice part."

That night I walked around the block repeatedly with Nick. I was so angry, I wanted to dig up shrubs, pull up weeds, chop down a tree, and break something. I had a choice name for my dad, several to be exact. I was in shock and seethed while anguish tore at my heart. How could he have done this to my baby? How could he have deceived me? What all had he done to her? Where was my mom when this happened? Did she leave Holly when she told me that she would watch her? What kind of person would do this? Who were my parents really? They felt like strangers, people I had no concept of, like I never knew them. The past year of Dad's coffee times with me, the gifts and help now seemed like a sick, perverted joke. Obviously, my father had a thing for little girls, and obviously my mother was either out to lunch on what was going on or in deep denial.

I recalled how last summer we brought the kids to their apartment to swim. Mom and Dad had decided to sell their riverfront home and try to find something across the river in the adjoining state. Retirement benefits were better there, and they would be closer to their aging parents. They rented a two-bedroom apartment while the condo they had purchased was being built. Grandpa John, my mother's eighty-nine-year-old father, lived in the apartment next door. My father's mother, Grandma Dena, lived a block away in a senior assistance apartment. It was a convenient move for all of them. Their new apartment had all the amenities: hot tub, weight room, a heated pool, and all within walking distance of the mall.

My dad, Nick, and the kids went for a swim while Mom and I decided to walk over to the mall to shop. On the way out of the complex, Mom commented on two young teenagers in swimsuits heading for the pool. "Hmm, Dad will enjoy the view."

I was taken aback at her remark. "Mom, they are but babies. They're only thirteen to fourteen years old!"

She did not respond. At the time, I found her remark odd, but now I was worried. Our eldest daughter, Ann, was close to those girls' age.

Ann had never stayed with my parents when she was small. We had lived out West at the time; she was six before she stayed with them, and her older brothers would often accompany her. Regardless, I felt a growing concern. Ann had mentioned that one time when she was watching cartoons while sitting on Grandpa's lap; he had inadvertently dropped his hand between her legs. He hadn't touched her inappropriately, but it made her uncomfortable. She asked him to move his hands, and he did. But then, after a while, his hand would slip, and she would have to move it or ask him to move it again.

At the time, I thought Dad was being insensitive. I told her no more sitting on his lap since he had disregarded her feelings. That had resolved the problem. Now it gnawed at me. It was enough to cause me to want to have Ann checked out and, of course, Holly too. I needed to know that Dad had not tried anything else during the times Ann had been at her grandparents' for sewing lessons with Mom or there to play with her cousins.

In the morning, I made an appointment with Child Protection Services to have both our girls checked at their child examination center.

CHAPTER 5

CHILD PROTECTION SERVICES

THE LADIES AT the Child Protection Services Child Investigation Center gave me a stack of forms. They required information about everything but my blood type. Ann was taken into a room first, and I was left in the waiting room, filling out forms while tending to Holly and baby Phoebe.

When it was Holly's turn, she was afraid to go. I reassured her that I would be there if she needed me and to tell them the truth about the "monster." She saw that Ann had returned with a large, white teddy bear and some snack treats; so she mustered up the courage to leave my side. An hour later, she came out with a teddy bear and a snack pack too. Now it was my turn. Ann would sit with Holly and Phoebe while the CPS staff talked with me.

I was taken to a room with a hidden microphone and a two-way mirror. They questioned me about why I had brought the girls and asked for the details of my nieces' disclosures, since they were examined at a different CPS office. I was then grilled on how I had questioned Holly and Ann and how they had responded. They asked if anything had ever happened to me. Then they told me that Holly had only disclosed that her grandpa was a monster, and while it was apparent "something" had happened, they didn't know what. They instructed me to follow up with a counselor, indicating that it may lead to her disclosing more in a professional setting and that professional testimony would be necessary if my father was prosecuted.

Ann had told them about Grandpa dropping his hands between her legs while sitting on his lap watching cartoons. She also told them that he had done this more than once. I had only been aware of one incident, but he had supposedly been attempting to break down her sense of boundaries, a process known as "grooming," causing her to become accustomed to his slow advances. He had sexually harassed Ann, but nothing beyond that had happened. I felt a huge relief; yet I was angered at his attempts to "groom" her.

Then they continued to question me. Had the girls been immunized? Were they up-to-date? When was their last well-child checkup? Do they see the dentist regularly? Do we spank our children? What forms of correction do we use? Do we have any guns in our home? Where do they go to school? When did they stay with my parents and how often? Am I in contact with my parents? When was the last time I spoke with them? And again they asked precisely what I had asked the girls. They asked how the girls had responded and what I had told them about coming to the examination center.

Following the questioning, I was instructed not to talk about the abuse or give any "leading" questions. CPS said there could be issues of "false memory" and that leading questions could plant a false memory. I had never heard of such a thing. How could you have a false memory? Wouldn't that be more like a delusion? And delusional people don't even know they're delusional; they don't even question if their memory is false.

I didn't get it. *Leading questions, false memory?* I pondered. *What were they insinuating? Did they think I would lead my daughters to tell me, "Yes Grandpa touched me?" Why would I want them to have memories of my father abusing them? Why would I want to twist something into making my father a pedophile? Why would I concoct some story and then request that my daughters be privately questioned and examined by strangers just so I could turn in their grandfather? I had loved and trusted my father for the past forty years! What kind of people would make up such sick stories anyway? Moreover, why would anyone suggest such a thing to a mother reeling with the shock of her father becoming a "monster" that sexually abused her nieces, sexually harassed her older daughter, and did "something" to her four-year-old?*

19

I was then told to take the girls for routine well-child checkups (never mind if our insurance didn't pay for the $200+ well-care visits). I was instructed not to spank them (which I rarely did and never with the older children); the CPS stated it was legal in the state, but they felt it was harmful and that only time-outs should be enforced. They offered referrals for setting up counseling appointments, which I declined. I had already set up an appointment for counseling with Grace prior to bringing the girls to CPS. Then they informed me that the girls had been examined without clothing; they had been questioned if anyone had hurt the body part that was being examined, and that the girls had responded "no" to the questions.

While my mind argued with my heart about all the rational reasons for their questions and cautious instructions, I couldn't shake the feeling of having been interrogated and scrutinized as a criminal, rather than receiving the compassion due a victim. Their findings, or lack of them, would be sent on to the county district attorney (DA), and the investigative sheriff would be giving me a call. We all left feeling humiliated. For the girls, being undressed by strangers was enough. For me, the fact that I was the mother of children that may have been harmed by my father made them consider me "less competent" and a possible suspect who needed evaluating.

After the appointment, I was afraid to talk with the girls about anything remotely associated with Grandpa. Holly began to mention the "monster" more. Because I felt intimidated that somehow I might be leading her by responding, I simply said nothing or said, "A monster?"

When I repeated this response several more days, Holly got mad at me and yelled, "You know, Momma, the monster that is Grandpa!"

I realized that when she spoke of the monster, my silence, out of fear of talking about the abuse, was frustrating her. My silence was invalidating her feelings and causing her to feel abandoned. I hoped our appointment with the counselor would help me understand what they meant by leading questions and false memory plants. Somehow there had to be a way to talk about the monster that brought a sense of comfort to Holly, versus a stoic silence based in the fear of leading her with a question.

CHAPTER 6

THERAPY

GRACE'S OFFICE WAS forty minutes from our house. The office had a grass yard behind it and pretty flowers along the walkway in front. The waiting room was well-stocked with a variety of toys and a small adjacent kitchen with complimentary beverages. Grace crouched down on her knees to get eye level with Holly and introduced herself. Holly played with toys in the waiting room while I spoke privately with Grace, filling her in on what had happened. Then she invited Holly to come in with us. She invited me to stay in the session until Holly felt comfortable being left alone with her. Holly started playing with the toys in Grace's office and wanted me to stay in the chair off to the side. By the next appointment, I was able to move the chair farther away from Holly, and by the third appointment, she felt safe enough for me to stay in the waiting room.

Grace explained that while she would meet with Holly only once a week, Nick and I would be with her every day. If Nick and I were trained in Play Therapy, we could help Holly process any abuse or trauma and help her recover quicker. Grace offered to train us once she could organize a small class. She asked if I thought Travis and Ellen would be interested.

I told Travis about Grace and the training class, and he contacted Mom to see if she would pay for his daughters' counseling and the class. She agreed to, so Travis arranged to bring Kristine and Diana to see

Grace. After meeting Grace, both he and Ellen agreed to participate in Grace's Play Therapy training class.

Travis had been financially dependent on Mom and Dad, which had created a significant tension. He vacillated from anger over what happened to his daughters and a deep sense of betrayal to a perceived need for their continued financial and emotional support. I was hopeful. Perhaps there would be healing for Travis as well as his family; perhaps this would be some of the good that would come out of the evil.

Travis made it through only half of the classes. Ellen had to finish them without him. Nick and I completed all the classes with baby Phoebe tagging along. After the classes ended, Travis and Ellen attempted a few Play Therapy sessions at home with their daughters and then gave up. Mom had informed Travis that Dad's attorney instructed her to stop paying for the counseling, but they could continue to supplement Travis's meager income since it was what they were doing prior to the "accusations."

In the end, their support of Travis made his daughters' accusations appear suspect, as though it was a ploy to get more money from our parents. At the time, Travis didn't realize this, and later it would become an issue in my father's investigation. It would be an argument Dad's attorney would use and one of the reasons the DA would give for minimizing the charges against Dad.

Grace offered to drop her fees and work with whatever Travis could afford. Kristine and Diana came for a few more counseling appointments, but they stopped coming altogether when the continual dysfunction that impeded healing in their home finally took over.

After completing the training, we began Play Therapy with Holly at home. Play Therapy gave her a way to remove any trauma from a first-person scenario. In Play Therapy she had a controlled world where she had the toys act out events and feelings as though they had happened to them and not to her. For her to talk about abuse directly was like reliving the event and could be traumatic, but in Play Therapy, the events were expressed incrementally and on her own timeframe. In Play Therapy there was no direct questioning, but rather a parent or therapist "reflecting back" as an emotional mirror, mimicking the child's feelings and mannerisms. If the parent or therapist does more than reflect, the child senses the inferences and will adapt his or her expressions to please authority. This removes a child's sense of control and will hinder the recovery process.

Due to the Play Therapy training, we understood that when children are questioned about traumatic events, they will admit to having been harmed and in the next breath deny it; the direct questioning is too close to the trauma for them to handle it emotionally. Children are geared for survival, and denial helps them to survive by removing them from an event.

Children need security and will protect those they depend on from anything that causes instability (in their lives). Therefore, a parent or caregiver must remain unemotional and neutral when a child begins to reveal that they have been sexually abused or harmed by another. Children desire to please, and if questioned improperly, they will tell an adult what they think the adult wants to hear rather than what is true. However, a fictitious or imagined event tends to break down in a short time and becomes apparent. It will not sustain in therapy the same way as a true event.

Children express their world through their play. Whatever happened to Holly would surface in her Play Therapy sessions with Grace and at home with us. And it did. The sense of control she felt in Play Therapy would also enabled her to talk about the abuse, as she felt ready, in a more direct manner. Through bits, pieces, and reoccurring themes, her fears and their source would unravel.

CHAPTER 7 ❧

"TRIGGERS" AND "POKIES"

"TRIGGERS" ALSO BECAME an accurate way for us to further understand what had happened to Holly. Triggers are non-threating objects or sensations that stimulate the release of a traumatic memory. Past trauma comes into consciousness with all the sensations and emotions of the original experience. To the victim, triggering feels as if the trauma is being relived, similar to a veteran who panics because of a flashback when a car misfires. A trigger could be a smell, taste, sound, color, texture, voice, place, person, food, picture, sensation, feeling, etc.

For weeks the biggest trigger for Holly seemed to be a bowel movement. She would fight a bowel movement for days, doing everything from bouncing up and down on a chair to refusing to use the restroom until she soiled her pants. When she could no longer withhold her bowel, she would scream as though in pain while it passed. There were no bloody or hard stools and no external hemorrhoids. She would scream for medicine, and I would use ointment on a bottom that appeared fine.

A year earlier, she was occasionally troubled by her bowels. She would call me to the bathroom, telling me her bottom hurt, when she had gone potty and to get medicine, but just as before, I saw nothing of concern. In the past when she had these rare episodes, I would follow up with increased fluid and fiber in her diet. Now her reactions had grown in intensity, and she was resistant to using the restroom at all.

One afternoon as she began to soil her pants, I scooped her up and carried her to the toilet. She went into a frenzy, clawing and screaming at me as though I was a monster. I wrapped my arms around her and held her tightly, letting her hit and claw. As I held her and the turmoil eased, she passed the stool.

She was still sobbing and crying when the phone rang. It was Angela, she felt prompted to call and check on how we were doing. I told her about Holly and the struggle I was having with her in the bathroom. She could hear Holly crying in the background and asked if she could speak with her. The call was divinely timed and a good diversion.

I asked Holly if my friend Angela could talk with her and Holly nodded. Angela explained to Holly that bad feelings were hurting her inside and that she would feel better if she got them out. Holly told Angela that a monster had hurt her. Angela asked the monster's name.

Holly said, "Grandpa."

Angela encouraged Holly to tell me what monster "Grandpa" had done, and that if she did, she would feel better. Holly calmed down and then handed over the phone. I thanked Angela for her kindness and call, then picked up Holly and rocked her in the rocking chair.

"Honey, why don't you want to go poopies?"

"Because monster poked me!"

"Monster poked you?" I reflected as in Play Therapy.

"Yes, Mommy, monster poked me in my poopie parts!"

"Monster poked you in your poopie parts, hmm? What did monster poke you with?"

"Monster poked me with a 'pokie,' and it really hurt!" she yelled out "really hurt" and sobbed. I prayed, asking God what I should do or say to help her process the memory and feel comforted. I sensed God's presence around us and felt urged to get a piece of paper.

"Can you draw Mommy a picture of the pokie?"

She picked up the pen and attempted to make what I thought could be the beginnings of a finger or penis. Frustrated, she handed me the pen. "I can't do it, Mommy. You draw it."

How was I supposed to know what to draw? I did my best to imitate what I thought she was attempting to draw. First I drew a finger shape, and then I drew a generic penis shape.

"No, no Mommy, not like that—a pokie!"

She grabbed at my hand and then dragged the ink pen the full length of the paper in a long line and put a small line horizontally across the top. It looked like a knitting needle or a hat pin.

"A pokie, Mommy!"

"Oh, a pokie." I again reflected, hoping she would feel understood even though I felt perplexed. "I am so glad you told Mommy this."

On the outside I remained calm, but on the inside, I felt distraught. *A pokie, God, he used a pokie! He used a pokie, and now she is afraid to go potty! What sick things did he do to her, God? What has happened to our sweet, innocent little girl?*

We rocked more as I held Holly until she was peaceful. She would still be troubled by her bowels but not with the same severity or the screaming. For several months, she would need me to hold her hand while she went, but now that the bad feelings were out, the fear of going and remembering became more manageable for her.

In spite of the horror I was feeling, I realized that God had directed me to grab paper and have her draw. Drawing was similar to Play Therapy in that it was one step removed from a direct first person retelling. It was a controlled surface, a blank box where she could create a picture that was separate from her but told the part of her story that she wanted told. Drawing became one of the greatest tools Holly would use to share what had happened to her. When triggered, she could quickly place her experience on paper, which helped her come back into the present while still releasing the past. Her artistic bent preferred drawing instead of Play Therapy, so from then on, we kept paper by the rocking chair.

The day after her pokie disclosure, I called the CPS Child Investigation Center and told one of the ladies that examined Holly about what she had said. The lady told me that sometimes children give names for things based on how it felt, and Holly probably meant that what had happened *felt* like being poked. I explained to her how Holly had drawn a picture of the pokie, but she remained convinced that it was just her way of saying how it felt.

These were the people who had instructed me not to talk with Holly about the abuse due to a fear of implanting false memories. However, when a child did speak of abuse, they had their own interpretations of what memories were acceptable. They had a mental box for the kinds of things they would accept had happened to children and the kinds of things they would not. In a sense, it seemed like *they* were the ones creating false information or "memories;" anything that took on a deeper level of perversion was in question or subject to their own "leading" interpretation.

In the future, I would see this mindset not only with the CPS but also within the legal investigation and prosecution process. I was sure Holly knew what she meant. The pokie was not a feeling, but a thing. She had drawn it. To believe otherwise would be twisting and leading her memories rather than accepting what she disclosed at face value. It would be doing the very thing I was instructed not to do.

CHAPTER 8

BAND-AIDS

IN SPITE OF feeling as if my world had stopped, daily life continued. On my shopping day, Holly insisted on coming along, while my eldest son, Joseph, watched the other children. Holly did not want to leave my side for a moment. She waited outside the bathroom door for me, followed me from room to room, and tagged along for my errands. Her fear for her own safety and for mine had increased. She was sure the monster would hurt one of us because she was "talking about" what he had done.

My first stop of the day was at the pharmacy to pick up a few items. Holly saw some Garfield cartoon Band-Aids that were twice the price of the generic brand. She wanted me to get them.

"No, honey," I told her, "the other Band-Aids are only a dollar and work just as well. Those are expensive; they cost three dollars."

She didn't complain but quietly put them back and moved down the aisle next to me.

When I went to the front of the store to pay, a man entered through the glass doors near the register. He was wearing carpentry-type Carhartt overalls and tan leather boots, had a brown, trimmed beard, and brown hair. I turned to pay and saw him reach toward Holly, handing her a small paper sack.

"Here, honey, these are for you."

"What's that?" I swung around protectively.

He smiled at me with eyes full of tenderness and gently responded, "I saw her looking at them and thought she should have them."

I glanced down at Holly and asked her to give me the bag. Inside were the Garfield Band-Aids. I looked up again, and the man was nowhere in sight. It had all happened so quickly, and it seemed he had just disappeared. Stunned, I turned the box over; on the front, above Garfield, were the words "Stick with me." I choked up and began to cry.

I was very protective of Holly, especially because we had been so horribly betrayed. I had become increasingly vigilant and aware of anyone near her or watching her. I had not seen the man anywhere around us the whole time we were in the small pharmacy. In fact, I had seen him walk in only as we were paying, then he was gone. Now I had Band-Aids for a hurt little girl and a message for me: "Stick with me." The disciples had not always recognized Jesus. Had I just done the same? This was no ordinary carpentry worker, and this was no ordinary cartoon Band-Aid box.

When Holly was done with the Band-Aids, I held on to the box. It sat on our fireplace mantle for the next year and is now a treasured keepsake.

CHAPTER 9

THE QUILT

LATER THAT SAME week, Mom called. She asked if she could quickly stop by and give me something she had made. She had hoped to have it completed for Nick's and my anniversary but had not completed it in time. Dad would not be in the car with her, and she would not come in. She would call on her cell phone as she pulled into the driveway so I could meet her at the door.

I had told her earlier that it was too upsetting for the children to see her right now, as they associated Mom with Dad. They knew Dad had hurt Travis's girls. She seemed to understand and told me she would wait until I felt it was okay for her to see the children.

I had not told her that Holly had been hurt by Dad, but after Holly's recent disclosure, I knew I would need to soon. I could feel a tension building between us, especially as I was trying to sort out what to think of her. Was she aware and in denial like Angela's mother-in-law, or was she innocent and deceived by Dad like we had been? I knew she was being untruthful all the times she had assured me she would babysit Holly and then left her with Dad. She may have felt I was too protective and saw no harm in leaving Holly while running a short errand.

From now on, however, our contact would be limited to occasional, private phone calls. Holly needed to feel safe to talk about Grandpa with the counselor and me. If she saw Mom or knew that I was talking with her, she would assume that Dad was close by.

Mom pulled up, and I quietly cracked open the door as she handed me a gift box. I thanked her and closed the door, relieved that the children had not been aware she had come. I took the box up to my room, shut the door, and opened it. Inside was a beautiful heirloom quilt of soft blue and yellow prints that matched my bedroom. She had trimmed it in my great grandmother's tatted lace and crocheted pieces from her special collection of needlework that had been passed on to her over the years. I was speechless. I sat and carefully admired the delicate work, and then I cried.

Was the gift really a reflection of her love? I so wanted it to be. I wept over the changes that had come in our relationship. This had to have been made by my "real mom," the part of her I so rarely saw. I wanted to believe that Dad had tricked Mom, that she felt trapped, and that she wanted me to know her love and comfort. Yet, I knew I couldn't accept this gift, at least not now. It was too beautiful and special to associate such a treasured heirloom with this troubled time.

I carefully repackaged the quilt, took it down to the mail center, and then sent her an e-mail. I told her how beautiful the quilt was and how I felt love in every stitch. I affirmed my affection for her and gratitude that she would make such a gift for me. I told her I was shipping the quilt to her for her to store in her closet or cedar chest and to give it to me at a different time. It was a treasure that I wanted to associate with better memories than the situation we were both dealing with. I shared how sorry I was that she was suffering in all this too. It was then that I informed her that Holly had also been harmed by Dad.

She sent a reply with a harsh tone, scolding me for having gone to others (my pastor and CPS) rather than confronting Dad first. She told me I had not gone about this in a biblical way and that she was concerned that Satan was having a heyday with me and my emotions. She said she was praying that all this would be sorted out and that I had never told her specifically what "I believed" Dad had done to Holly. Then she ended the e-mail by assuring me in large letters that she had "NEVER" left Holly alone with Dad.

What was I to think ... so you were there, Mom, and you let him hurt her?

I replied that I was having a hard time understanding who she and Dad really were. She then responded, reassuring me that they were the same parents who had always loved me. This was their love? Deception, abuse, betrayal ... I found no comfort in a "love" so painfully twisted.

I was thankful the quilt was not on my bed and that I had shipped it back to her. Perhaps it had only been part of the deceit. I didn't know what to think. My nights were wrapped in enough grief. Who was my mom? On the one hand, she had spent hours making a beautiful, loving gift for me. On the other, she had been present while my father used a pokie on my sweet, innocent, little Holly.

CHAPTER 10 ❧

SEVERING TIES

MOM CONTINUED TO send e-mails and cards with birthday money for the children. At first, she and Dad both signed them, and I promptly sent them back. I e-mailed her and explained that I could not give the children cards or checks with Dad's signature and asked her to stop sending them. Then she would mockingly cross out his name and write hers in big letters, as if to say, "See, this makes it okay," and resend them to me.

For seven months, she would continue to send notes with Scriptures and birthday cards in spite of my request for her to stop. Her e-mails were "just to inform me" that so-and-so had passed on and I should send a card to the address she included. She would also "inform" me to pray for my eldest brother, Wendell, regarding his next mission trip, conservative political endeavors, or legal battles. When I stopped responding to the e-mails, she would print them off and send them by mail.

The last note I actually read from her said: "My dear daughter, the silence between us rips at my heart. Each day that passes seems to pull us farther apart. Every morning I ask the Lord to heal hearts and by His love and grace restore our family. I long to hear your voice and to see you, to hug my grandchildren again. It is my prayer that you will one day forgive me for my unkind and critical words. May you know that I love you dearly and that I will always love you. Please let me know when it will be okay for me to call or visit again, with love, your Mom." And she included the Scripture James 3:18.

She also sent newly-released Christian books and encouraged me to read them, hoping it would "help" me. Often times the phone would ring and the person on the other end would not respond and not hang up. I began to feel suspicious of the frequent "wrong numbers" we seemed to be receiving. I changed our e-mail and our phone number. I wrote "return to sender" on the cards she sent the children and returned her e-mails unopened. Eventually she stopped trying.

In what would be the last phone call I would have with her, I clarified that if we both went to counselors and they deemed it was in our best interest to meet or talk, we could. Until then, it was too painful to have any communication. She refused to get counseling, saying it was impossible, with no explanation as to why.

Travis's relationship with Mom remained the same. He continued to stay in touch with her, and she continued to help him pay the bills. He felt protective of Mom and believed that she had been deceived by Dad. He would let Mom take Kristine out shopping for clothes, because he didn't want Mom to feel bad. It wasn't her fault Dad had done this.

Travis slept and cried through Christmas that year. "It just isn't the same without Mom and Dad," he said. And then he fell apart as the children opened the presents Mom had dropped off. I understood the perceived loss, and I felt it too. But how did it make Kristine feel to see him weeping over the loss of Dad's presence, the man who had repeatedly raped her? How did she feel as her father continued to cling to the wife of this man and feel sorry for her at Kristine's expense? My heart ached for Kristine. Travis just didn't get it, and I wondered if he ever would.

When Kristine was younger, there were so many times I wanted to take her home with me and raise her. Once, she had stayed the night at our house for a sleepover with Ann. Afterwards, she wrote me a thank you note, saying, "I love you, Auntie Hannah. I love you so much that I want to go home with you. So much so that I want to go with you everywhere."

Now I understood that it was more than just a thank-you note of affection. Her home had not felt safe, and the grandparents that were supposed to bring more stability into her life were the very ones who brought more destruction. Now the card's message made me cry.

Kristine had started to act out sexually with her younger siblings and with other kids at school. As much as I wanted to ask Ellen to let Kristine stay with us, I could not with younger children in our home.

CPS was making follow-up visits to Travis's, which was good for the children. Travis's family was receiving county services, which included fifteen free counseling sessions, but there was no consistency in the counseling for Kristine. CPS insisted they keep their home cleaner. Ellen had taken their baby into the clinic, and he was diagnosed with parasites due to animal feces. Kristine was doing poorly in school and repeatedly being suspended. Travis and Ellen were told that they had to improve their parenting and living situation or risk having their children placed in someone else's care. Due to CPS's visits and the school district's involvement, Travis became more restricted in his contact with Mom, which was good, especially for the children.

CHAPTER 11 ❧

PINS

MORE OF THE harm that happened to Holly was being exposed. She felt safer knowing her grandparents were no longer a part of her life, and she began to express things throughout her day in play or in strange, out-of-nowhere comments. While coloring in a *Toy Story* coloring book, she remarked, "See, Mommy, I colored Woody. He has a big pee-pee; he keeps it in his pants. Do you have a big pee-pee?"

"No, honey, Mommy is a girl. I don't have a big pee-pee."

While playing with a stuffed dog, she asked for diaper wipes. "He doesn't like red," she said, as she repeatedly wiped the back end of the toy dog.

Then one morning, after using the bathroom, she came running to me all excited. "Mommy, Mommy, the pokie came out; come see!"

I followed her to the bathroom and found a small, thin, ¼-inch twig floating in her urine. It could have easily fallen there by the shake of a carpet or the emptying of a shoe. I wasn't sure a pokie had come out. This was a small twig. When I asked about the pokie in the picture she had drawn being a big pokie and the pokie in the potty being a small one, she told me that Grandpa had big pokies and little pokies. The little pokies were in the hole by her "pee-pee" part (which she animatedly pointed to), but now "it had come out." The big pokie had poked her poopie part, not her other part.

36

I then recalled how months earlier one of Holly's nightmares was unsettling. She came into our room in the middle of the night and said that a monster had poked her by her pee-pee part. Nick and I didn't know what to think of the dream, and I simply tucked her in next to me to comfort her.

That evening, once the children were in bed, I went online. I typed in "vaginal inserts," "pins," "twigs," etc., trying to make sense of little pokies. The disgusting sites one can find with such terms were sickening. I just wanted to understand what was necessary but not feel slimed in the process. I came across a site that talked of curse pins (small twigs) that were inserted in sick, dark, sexual rituals and looked like what had floated in our toilet earlier. I further read that pins or "shots" are used in ritual abuse. They can easily be inserted into sensitive areas to create intense pain without leaving any visible marks.

That night, I didn't sleep much at all. Once again, the questions tossed in my mind. *Who is my father, and what is he into? What has he done to Holly? Did he stick things inside her? Is he a part of some of this sick perversion that I came across on the Internet?* I wanted to vomit. I needed help; I needed to talk to someone who knew about the use of pokies and the evil associated with them. I needed to know what to do and what we were dealing with.

CHAPTER 12 ❧

A TRIP TO CANADA

THE NEXT MORNING I called Colette Jacobs at Ellel Ministries in Calgary, Canada, and told her of Holly's disclosures. She told me that children do not make up this sort of thing and that Edna Peach, one of their top instructors and ministers, knew about the use of pins in sexual abuse and could help. Edna would be teaching there that weekend and would then be flying back to England.

"Can you get on a plane with Holly and come immediately? You can stay at our house," said Colette.

In a whirlwind, I used our credit card to purchase the flight tickets, packed our suitcases, collected documentation for customs, and with Holly and baby Phoebe in tow, we caught a flight to Canada the next morning.

When we landed in Calgary, Colette's husband, Andrew, was there to meet us with his warm car. It was in a parking lot surrounded by piles of snow. He helped secure the children's car seats, his eyes softening as he held Phoebe while I strapped in Holly. Andrew was quiet, but his gentle heart spoke volumes through his eyes. I swallowed hard to hold back the tears. I felt like I had come home to true family. Their house was a split-level, similar to the one we had owned on the West Coast. It was decorated in dated country style and mixed furnishings from the seventies through the nineties. Precious Moment figurines sat on shelves in the dining area with pictures of their daughter's wedding. Smaller photos were placed lovingly throughout the rest of the house. A table seating four was in the kitchen, and a family room with a welcoming fire in the fireplace was just on the other side of the room. Our bedroom was in the finished basement, with a full pine wood bedroom set from the sixties and was adjacent to a small bathroom across the hall.

I felt like I was in a haven—a place to take off my shoes and lie on the sofa pillow, knowing the afghan was for me to use. Colette went over things with me in the morning, and then they arranged a time to take me to meet Edna at the retreat center. Between our times with Edna, they prayed with Holly and me.

The next evening, Edna was available to meet with us. She spoke with me first and then prayed for Holly. Holly played with toys in the sitting area as I met with Edna. Phoebe began to fuss, and one of the women on staff asked if she could take her in the other room for me. I struggled with letting her out of my sight, but as soon as she was out of the room, she calmed down.

Edna sensed there was a level of spiritual warfare we were battling. She asked for the details of Holly's confessions and questioned me at length about the discovery of my father's abuse. After she had a clear understanding, she spoke to me about the use of pins in sexual rituals that mix the occult with perverted acts.

Speaking with authority, knowledge, and experience of an expert, she emphasized how serious the effects of these rituals are physically, spiritually, and psychologically. She explained how pins (curse pins) are used in conjunction with demonic rituals and the invoking of evil spirits to torment the victims. Curse pins leave no mark and are a challenge to locate (even with X-rays) due to a demonic component designed to keep them hidden. She had worked with victims where the Lord exposed the pins, miraculously dissolved them, or the victims had passed them without injury.

It seemed unreal to me, but then why would my four-year-old be so excited about a small stick in a toilet if she had not been the victim of such sickness? Where would she have heard of pokies that were put inside little girl's holes or believe that they had been in her and one had come out?

Edna explained how people who are deeply involved in this level of evil create flawless fronts to hide behind and work in groups and networks on many levels. My father hadn't just suddenly developed a sexual problem or a sick fixation; with his well-developed Christian front, he would have been secretly involved in this for years. It was the level of contrast between his Christian front and the uncovered abuse that indicated this had been ongoing for some time. Those deeply involved in evil strive to create contrasts to hide behind, often battling and working against the very evils they partake of in secret.

She then went on to caution me about Holly's safety. I needed to be very careful when I went places and to keep her close by when outside, even in our yard. She told me not to trust anyone with her at this vulnerable time and to be very careful with my mom.

"At this level of evil, your mom would have to be aware." Edna paused, leaned forward, and looked at me intently as though to steel me for what she was about to say next. "Your father is a very, very evil man. There is no way Holly could have made up any of the things she has told you, and you have only begun to understand all that your father has done. You will need to learn about some very difficult things in the days ahead to undo this."

Edna's words hit hard. The room seemed to spin, and I felt short of breath. In the future, I would need to delve into deeper levels of spiritual warfare: learn how to pray in a manner that would minister healing from the effects of trauma and sexual abuse and how to remove the demonic oppression from the rituals that were done to Holly. During the process, I would have to take a very difficult look at the depravity of mankind and the darkness of an Antichrist agenda that motivates its slaves.

Edna then left the room and joined Holly, plopping down on the floor without concern about her white business suit and engaging her in play. She talked with Holly and asked if she could pray with her. Holly responded positively as Edna gently addressed specific things the Lord directed her to pray and rebuked demonic oppression. Holly yawned a few times and remained peaceful.

Edna felt prompted to ask me if my father had ever taken a nap with Holly or spent any time with her in her bedroom. I thought for a moment and recalled when my parents came over to help out after

I returned home from the hospital. I was exhausted from delivering little Phoebe and went upstairs to rest. Mom had been making supper when I awoke and Dad had been "playing" with Holly in her room. She seemed fine at the time, but I had since learned that it didn't mean everything was *fine*.

Edna told me to get rid of Holly's mattress immediately; she would need a new one. The type of sexual spirits tied to the abuse Holly had experienced was of such a nature that the mattress would have to be removed. It could not be spiritually cleansed. She asked me to call Nick and have him remove it right away. Nick unquestioningly loaded Holly and Ann's mattresses into the back of our van that night. At some time in the past, we had switched Holly's mattress with Ann's because Holly's was firmer and we thought it would provide better support for Ann's frame. Two mattresses only a year old were taken to the dump. Edna also instructed me to begin going through our house and removing things my parents had given us as the Lord directed. The financial impact of this had only begun.

Disposing of the mattress reminded me of the story of Achan and the defeat of Israel at Ai (Joshua 6–7). God had told the Israelites not to keep any of the plunder for themselves when they defeated Jericho. Achan disobeyed and took some of the spoils. As a result, Israel suffered loss of lives and defeat in their battle at Ai. I knew from Scripture that one could not stand in battle with forbidden things taken from the enemy's camp. At times, the Israelites were permitted to take plunder; other times they had to destroy everything.

In Leviticus 14:33–57, God would mark the walls of a dwelling unclean with a fungus. The walls would have to be scraped and the house closed up for seven days. If the fungus returned, the house had to be destroyed. If it didn't return, a sacrifice was made, and the house was considered cleansed. Some things could be cleansed, and some could not. It was a mystery that involved their dependence on the Lord and their obedience to Him. I knew that all of Scripture was written for my equipping and instruction, and while I am not under Judaic law because of the final sacrifice of my Savior, Jesus Christ, I still live under spiritual law. Just as gravity is a physical law, there are spiritual laws that I may not fully understand, but respecting the One who created spiritual law makes a difference in the outcome of a battle.

Edna and the other staff at the Ellel Retreat Center had leaned on the Lord for wisdom in spiritual battles many times prior to our prayer. They knew there were situations where you are at the deep end of the pool and reliance on the Lord's leading is your only life preserver. While some people of the Christian faith may question the validity of the instructions we had been given, their questioning indicates a lack of experience themselves. I knew Edna had a theology that had been tested on the mission fields, in prisons, and in the forgotten places of the world. Otherwise, I would not have flown to Calgary. We were confident they knew what to do, and our confidence in this ministry had been proven years earlier in our lives.

Four years prior, our dear friends Jed and Lydia had come home on furlough from their overseas missionary work. Lydia called and was urgent in her tone; she needed to see us and asked if we could come visit them at their parents' mountain cabin. Their seminar schedule was full, as being on furlough often meant little rest for them, but they would be at the cabin visiting family for the weekend.

Jed had mentored Nick as a new believer and taught him the importance of studying the Word of God. Lydia had been an example of self-sacrifice, trustworthiness, and true friendship for me. Jed graduated from a well-known conservative seminary, and then went overseas to the market place of life in a nation steeped in idolatry and false beliefs. His denominational views fell short and were taken out of their boxes as he walked into a place of faith where the Word of God was his only survival manual.

They both realized how little their education had prepared them for people bound in idolatry and witchcraft. Lydia had once prayed for a local pastor who was suffering over the recent loss of his mother. As she prayed, he slipped out of his chair and slithered across the floor like a snake. She knew immediately that deeper insight was required for ministry—the insight that believed in the Word of God regardless of personal experiences or doctrinal views. The mission organization sent their whole team to acquire more tools for ministry at one of the Ellel Ministries training schools. Something had happened to Lydia during the training that she wanted to share with me in person. Nick took Friday off, and we drove up to the cabin to meet with them.

Lydia, radiant and glowing, told me what had happened to her while at Ellel. During the classes, she realized that there were demonic strongholds in her family line that were rooted through blood oaths and vows that her grandfather made in the secret occult and pagan rituals practiced in freemasonry. As she began to pray into these things during the training, God began to heal her physically. The cysts in her breasts that were precancerous and always needing to be rechecked shrank to nothing and were no longer a concern. The tooth infection that the doctor could not find an antibiotic to treat was instantly healed. The back pain and stiff neck from a car accident the year before was gone.

She urged us to go to the next training. She knew of the feminine problems and difficult pregnancies I had endured and the fact that my grandfather had been a thirty-third-degree mason. She wondered if some of the same things that were in her extended family were also in mine.

Nick and I prayed for months, set money aside, and went to Ellel's training. Once there, we found ourselves immersed in solid, biblical teachings while receiving safe, loving, powerful, personal prayer that dealt with the breaking and removal of family curses, vows, and their effects. We were rubbing elbows with those who had done laps in the deep end of the pool to rescue the drowning, and we left feeling rescued as well. Like Lydia, Nick and I returned home different. I no longer needed glasses or hormonal creams, and Nick had a new sensitivity to the direction and leading of the Holy Spirit. We felt lighter, and our passion for the Lord ignited. It was not an emotionally drummed-up passion, but one that resonated in the mundane of life as much as on the mountain top.

I left Ellel different this time as well, only I felt shaken and dazed, like I was being brought out of sleep with a bucket of ice water. I wanted to flee like Jonah had from Nineveh. I wanted to get on a different boat to another destiny, a boat that took me to a place where I didn't "need to learn about some very difficult things."

Who wants to even remotely know about such evil? What mother wants to wrap her mind around such darkness having been inflicted upon her child? What daughter wants to know that her father, who sat next to her in church, singing hymns, was secretly involved in instigating evil?

When Hitler was gassing the Jews, how many people wanted to know or even believe that civilized humanity was capable of causing such evil? It shook their worldview. Even today, there are those who pretend the Holocaust didn't happen, but it did. Who wants to know that there are trusted people who appear to be the salt of the earth and live two very separate lives? We want to believe that people who look and act good really are. However, I had to face the darkness and the evil deception that disguised it. I had to move forward for the sake of our little girl. I had to visit Nineveh.

CHAPTER 13 ❦

BARBIE AND BABIES

EARLY THAT SPRING, Nick felt I needed to get away with the children and do something fun. He rented a camping space at a nice RV park near the beach. The campground had an indoor pool, game room, laundry, showers, and convenience store. He drove our travel trailer to the campsite and set it up so I could spend the week with the children. He would join us for the weekend after work.

We played cards and swam. Holly seemed calmer because we were far away from where Grandpa knew we lived. Phoebe was enjoying the jabber of her sister, so I pulled out the skillet and began to heat up some supper. Holly drew with her magnetic board while Phoebe stretched and kicked on a quilt on the trailer floor.

"Look, Mommy, this is how they take the skin off."

Jolted by her comment, I reminded myself to "reflect back" and turned to see what she had drawn.

"Oh, this is how they take the skin off," I mirrored.

"Yep," she said and handed me her drawing. "They use a knife." Then, pointing to the fingers she said, "See the rubber band parts."

It was a primitive arm and hand shape with horizontal and vertical lines all across it. Then she abruptly turned away and asked if she could go outside to see Ann. I told her she could and instructed Ann to stay near the trailer with her while I finished fixing supper.

45

In a daze, I stirred the skillet. *How they take the skin off? What in the world did this mean?*

Back at home, I had tried to incorporate consistent Play Therapy into our week. Grace had suggested two to three times per week. I would play with Holly when Phoebe was napping or in the evening when Nick was home. Holly was to have thirty minutes of uninterrupted play. I had nurturing, domestic, violent, and building toys set around the room. These were toys I had purchased and were only to be used for our special play time. I would set the timer and play anything she wanted, anyway she wanted, as long as it didn't hurt either of us or damage the furniture in the room.

At first, she would bring out a mean-looking doll (like Darth Vader) and pile it under blocks or set it far off and then would return to her play. When playing with the dollhouse, she would continually act out the little doll getting sick, calling on the phone for help, saying that someone was dead or that her mommy was killed and she was all alone. Other times, she would take the dark figure called "Bad Grandpa" and smack him on the floor, breaking off a leg or an arm.

When she would play alone in her room, I would sneak a tape player under the bed, put a video camera in the corner, or use the baby monitor. During these times of playing alone, she would tell me that she wanted to close her door and that she didn't want her sister to come in their room. She would do this when she wanted to play "married" with the Barbie dolls, only it was a Kelly and a Ken.

She would make Ken say in a sickly-sweet voice, "You can marry me when you get bigger." Then she would change his voice to a harsh tone, "I will smack you if you don't lie down." The voice would then switch again to the sweeter one. "I will buy you a princess dress."

She would reenact this scene repeatedly when playing Barbie. Sometimes she would have the Barbies play out that they had to decide who was the prettiest, and the loser would go away sad or dejected. The play would end with a Barbie talking on the phone, asking for help because someone was killed. There was always a victim in her play, and Ken was always harsh and manipulative.

When I overheard her talking about the doll getting a princess dress if she cooperated with Ken, I recalled the princess dress my mom had brought over for her a few months before Phoebe was born. My mom had told me that she had promised Holly she would get it for her. It was a Snow White costume, complete with crown and sparkly red shoes. After Holly had put it on, my Mom asked her to sit so she could take a picture. Holly sat sideways and tucked her legs, striking a model's pose.

I was surprised at how quickly she responded to Mom and sat like a little model without instruction. I commented, "Look at her pose like in a movie. Where did she learn to do that?" Mom didn't respond.

Then one morning Holly decided that instead of playing married with Barbie she wanted to play married with her life-sized doll. She told Ann to stay out of their room, so Ann covertly turned on the baby monitor and left her alone. In that sickly-sweet voice she began telling the doll that when she got bigger she could marry her, similar to what she had played before with Ken and Barbie, and once again, her voice changed as she harshly said, "Lie down or I will hit you in the nose!" Then in the softer voice, "It is all right, honey, I will wipe you up."

Then she had the doll respond with a bizarre comment. "I like kissing on the lips, Jesus." Then once again in an angry voice she yelled, "You stupid Holly, I will kill that girl!"

This was not a normal little girl's doll play; this was the bits and pieces of something very sick.

During this time of playing "married," she began to express an extreme fear of men. Holly was now sleeping next to or in our bed every night. There were some nights where she was clingier, and the bed on the floor was too far away from me. She would want to tuck in next to me, but only with me between her and Daddy.

"I don't want to sleep by Daddy!" she would start hollering if she was moved over to the middle of the bed so I could sleep better and not worry about her rolling off.

I felt sad for Nick. Holly had gone from being "Daddy's little girl" to a baby just wanting her mother. Although he knew it wasn't about him, it still caused him pain. Tears would pool at the corner of his eyes. Would he get his little girl back? In his heart, he knew God would heal her, but the journey was uncertain, and the time it would take was unknown.

Holly had been afraid that since Grandpa was a man and Grandpa was a "scary" that maybe Daddy was a scary too. And since her big brothers looked like men, maybe they were "scaries" as well. Actually, all men were probably scaries. She would sometimes question me just to be sure I was a female.

"Momma, you are a girl, right?"

"Yes, honey, I am a girl."

"And I am a girl too."

"Yes, honey, you are a girl too."

"You're not a scary, right?"

"No, I am not a scary."

Daddy and her brothers went from being the men she tickled, hugged, snuggled, and read stories with, to being scaries. It would be months before she realized that just because they were men it didn't mean they were scaries.

Then one evening, Holly stunned me with a comment while I was bathing her baby sister. Leaning over the tub, she looked at Phoebe and saw me washing her using a washrag. It seemed to have triggered something, and out of nowhere she said, "It's all right, baby, we'll wipe up the blood." Then she turned to me and asked, "We don't break babies, right, Mommy?"

With waves of nausea building inside I gently responded, "No, we don't break babies; we love babies. Did you see a baby broken?"

"Yes, I saw a baby in the fire." She stood quiet for a second, stared vacantly at the floor, and then turned to run off and play.

That night, I sat in my room in the dark and sobbed. "God, a baby! A broken baby in the fire! What in the world is that?" I felt so overwhelmed, numbed by pain and anger, brokenhearted and afraid, all at the same time.

Then after the storm of my sobs, God's voice was clear as He kept saying in my heart, *"I am bigger than this."*

His words were an anchor that would keep me sane as I faced a darkness that felt like a massive Assyrian army led by a mocking Rab-shakeh, arrogant in his power and laughing at the belief in a God who could defeat him.

CHAPTER 14 ❧

"ROCKIE" TIME REVELATIONS

THE ABUSE HOLLY revealed first trickled and then gushed out as she felt safe and knew that Grandma and Grandpa were gone from our lives. It was as if a dam of emotions began to break in her. All the fear and feelings no longer needed to be hidden. Every day she would cry and scream due to triggering, and I didn't always know what would set her off. When she began an episode, I would quickly go to her, scoop her up in my arms, and rock her.

At the intensity of these moments, Play Therapy was not the avenue for her. Play Therapy had been a door with a key that said, "You are heard. You can say anything, and it is okay." It was a door that led to another level full of the releasing of trauma-based emotions.

At this level of anguish, she was reliving something so awful that it needed releasing quickly. She would holler for the paper by my rocking chair and would begin to calm as she would take up the pen and step back into a place she could control and would find relief at the same time. If she had difficulty drawing, she would tell me what to draw and then complete the picture herself, asking me to write down the words as she told me about the drawing. I would reflect back at what she was telling me, and she would feel relieved that the bad feelings and memories were now stored on her paper.

Sometimes this would not work. The severity of the triggers would be so great that she would thrash and yell repeatedly, "I can't talk about it!" She wanted to speak, but she was terrified by a fear of retribution from Grandpa and the demonic voice that threatened to physically torment her if she talked. She would scream, her head would roll back, and then she would pass out. When she regained consciousness, she would moan and act groggy as though drugged, and then she would sleep.

Other times, the emotions and terror she was feeling would remain and she would wake up screaming, reliving something I needed to help her process. I would wait for the Lord to reveal what I should say to comfort her or help her move past the moment and release the memory. I never knew where these moments would take us. There wasn't a book I could turn to for answers, and there wasn't anyone to call who could help us walk through this. There was Jesus, and He was my only pilot. He knew what Holly needed. All I knew was how dependent I was on Him for any sense of reality and direction.

Holly knew that when we snuggled in the rocking chair the bad feelings dissolved, and she would frequently ask to "rockie" with me.

One afternoon she came to me. "Mommy, I need to rockie. I need to draw a picture!" she cried. Quickly, she began to draw while I held her in my lap and waited.

"This is me in a dress with flowers on it. See the flowers, Mommy?"

"Yes, I see the flowers."

"This is the owie on my head. I have a headache, my leg hurts, I can't run very good. This is a scary, scary grandpa. I tried to get away. He was running after me. I was in a jungle, bushes and sand. He poked me with a pokey in my potty parts. Grandma went in the house and left me. You weren't there, Mommy; you left me, Mommy. You left me!" she yelled and then broke into a flood of sobs.

I held her close and explained, "Honey, if Momma knew Grandpa was going to hurt you, I would have never left you. I didn't know he was bad. Mommy didn't know. I am so, so sorry. I am here, honey. You are safe now, and I am not going to let him hurt you anymore."

She cried until she fell asleep in my arms, and then I wept. The pain in my heart was beyond words. To Holly, it was if I had abandoned her. How many times had she cried out for me and I didn't know? How many times had she needed me and wondered where I was and why I wasn't coming to get her? How young had she been when this horror began? My desire to be a good mother felt sabotaged and stolen, as if someone had ripped my child from my arms while I helplessly watched. As she relived the memories, it was as if I was watching it happen to her and unable to stop it. It was the past happening in the present, and I was living the trauma in reverse. I was tormented by the anguish of knowing she had called for me and needed me to protect her, but I wasn't there. I had left her, and she did not understand why.

Later, when I was downstairs, Holly yelled, "I am a little girl!"

I went upstairs and found her crying in her room. Once again, we rocked with paper in hand.

"Grandma is not a nice grandma! She hit me a lot, and Grandpa didn't help. He did a bad thing!" she yelled. Then crying she told me again, "You left me there. You left me there!"

I assured her with the same promises I had promised about my father, except now it was about my mother. I said, "I will not let Grandma hurt you anymore. I will keep you safe. You are not going to her house anymore. She cannot come over. I won't let her bother you."

My mother, like my father, also had the same outstanding Christian front. Besides her exemplary service in the General Assembly, she had written the counseling manuals for a national pro-life organization where she had served as a counselor and board member. She had opened pregnancy counseling centers and trained volunteers. She hosted missionaries and helped care for one missionary's daughter, Terra, when her father was traveling. She had served as a deaconess and had been active in supporting the Valley Christian School.

My mother was the one who prayed with me to receive the Lord when I was five. I had seen a Christmas play at church and wanted to know what was so special about baby Jesus and why he had come to earth.

"Jesus is God's Son who came as a baby to the earth. When he was a man, he died on a cross for people's sins."

"Why did He have to die for sins?"

"So He could take the sin away, and people could go to heaven with Him."

I asked if I could pray, and in childlike faith, I asked Jesus to take away my sins, and I thanked Him for coming to earth to die on a cross for me. I asked Him to be with me and take me to live with Him in heaven someday. My mother was the one who helped me form the words that forever changed me, but had those words ever really formed in her?

Now she was a stranger to me and worse. In the months ahead, Holly would reveal to me how my mom held Holly down for my father, took her to sick places, participated in harming her, and mocked her. I would learn that my mother was not in denial with a sick man but that she was sick too and part of the evil in which he was involved. She was a participant and aided him in their joint life of evil deception. While my little Holly screamed and cried, my mother watched my father enjoy himself, and then she would do the cleanup and afterwards give Holly treats. I couldn't conceive how she could do this or how he could find such behavior stimulating.

In order to learn more about pedophiles, I did research and tried to make sense of something that was inconceivable. I learned that pedophiles can have sexual release while a child screams in pain, struggles to get away, and cries, begging the offender to stop. It doesn't affect them. A pedophile's view of a child is based on false reality. They consider the child as either a willing participant that deserves or desires the abuse or as a means for the gaining of a sense of power.

When pedophiles are exposed, there are usually additional, unknown victims. They generally don't stop at one victim. Not to expose or report offenders is to allow their crimes to proliferate. The more they abuse, the more they become pros at disguise, grooming, and deception. Only a small percentage of pedophile offenders ever admit their crimes.

They can molest a child in a brief second with a quick grab or touch; it takes so little time to do so much damage. Small children (infants to age five) appear to be the preferred victims. Adults forget that small children do not think as they do. Pedophiles understand this and know they can easily confuse and silence a child who does not know how to process or explain the harm that has taken place.

Over time, the emotions or images of the past come to the surface when the child (or now a grown adult) no longer perceives him or herself to be vulnerable or small. The memories can first release as an emotion with no source (such as a panic attack) or in emotionless pictures that seem disconnected or as triggers that are bigger than life, and suddenly, they are reliving it in the here and now. Usually the bomb goes off in adulthood. By God's grace, Holly was dealing with things now.

CHAPTER 15 ❧

ASHES AND
TEA CUPS

I WALKED A lot more those days; it helped with the anger and the trauma I was watching unfold. It was a way I could pour my heart out to the Lord away from the children. New construction was going on in our neighborhood, and as I passed a newly-framed house, the smell of fresh-cut pine was in the air. Tears welled up. The scent of fresh pine was the scent of my father when I was young. It was the smell of cut lumber clinging to his flannel shirt when he would come in off a construction site, the smell of the lumber as I would pound nails when he let me come along to help.

Now it was the smell of something lost, ending, and no more. Everything I knew of my father, everything I believed, was gone, but how do you grieve what you are no longer certain ever existed? I could only grieve over what I thought he was or once believed him to have been. I had lost my father, but there was no funeral and no memorial. He was gone, and nothing but questions, anguish, and anger were left in his place. Now I was beginning to wonder if his wife was my real mother at all. What had happened to her? What had my father done to the part of her I called my "real mom"? I began to associate both of them with the scent of ashes as I burned all the letters Mom had written over the years and the cards they gave us as well.

I had heirlooms in every room, and they were constant reminders of my parents. The vase on the mantle, the English Roses bone china, the hutch, the tatted doilies, the mantle clock, the cedar chest, the crystal pieces, the decorator plates, the various pieces of antique furniture, the vintage linens and hats, the jewelry, the old books, the crocheted bedspread, and the teacups.

There were numerous teacups. Mom and Dad had brought them back from their last RV trip. They had purchased them from a variety of antique shops, estate sales, and secondhand stores all across the Midwest and Upper East Coast. I had mentioned to Mom before they left on their trip that I wanted to collect tea cups for the girls. She said she would keep an eye out for some. During the trip, she decided she would collect them too and perhaps even sell them. She bought box after box.

For weeks they were examined, priced, and sorted. I helped Mom look up the year and value of her collection. Some were quite valuable, and I learned as I helped her how to determine Japanese look-alikes from authentic English bone china. I could tell a Shelly from a Paragon without picking it up. Some cups were dated in the early 1800s, and some were from Belgium, Bavaria, and Ireland. Several were in complete sets of four or six and in pristine condition. It was a memory we shared, and it started my collection and established the girls' collections.

One evening, Nick came home and found me weeping amongst bits of china shards in the garage. I had broken some of the cups and a creamer from Ireland. I would be selling the rest on consignment.

"Look, it's like my life. What's real anymore? Who are these people who raised me, who are they?"

Nick picked me up and held me. "We are real and our children are real and what we have is real."

Breaking the cups felt good for a second, but it wasn't enough. I could have broken everything, and it wouldn't change what was true.

Between the classified ads and a consignment shop, I unloaded all of the heirlooms. The lady at the shop was pleased to take the bedspread and vintage linens. She liked the collection of old books my father had given me over the years, but she cautioned me, "They don't fetch much of a price, but I will take them. I have too many teacups. Maybe in April you could bring them back; they'd be good for Mother's Day."

"Okay, I will bring them back before May."

I felt numb as I left the shop. These items were merchandise to her, and rightly so, but to me they had once been heirlooms with memories of the people who had given them. Now all the memories were questions.

"It's just stuff, really," I swallowed hard and told myself. But the "stuff" represented a part of my life that was gone, shattered like the cream pitcher from Ireland and the china cups from England. How can you pass on items that come from a pedophile and his abusive wife? None of my kids would ever want them, and besides, I could not give them the things that now seemed cursed.

The kids wanted to pretend I had different parents or that I came from an orphanage. It was a horror to Holly to think that the "monster" was also my father. I told her God was my Daddy, my only Daddy.

CHAPTER 16 ❧

"NAKED LADY" AND FRIENDS

IT HAD BEEN a while since Holly had played with anyone her age, and we both needed a fun day. Every day was Play Therapy, "rockie" moments, and adapting to a myriad of triggers related to being poked, molested, and violent horror. Holly steadily increased in the details as she felt unrestricted and was able to express with a growing vocabulary, so the difficulty in hearing what she was sharing also increased for me. I longed for a less heavy day for her sake and mine.

A good friend from the homeschool co-op, Donna, had called the day before to ask if the children could get together and play. She needed some advice on homeschooling her son Paul. He was challenging to work with, and she wanted to know what I had done with my older boys. Her daughter Cora was Holly's age and was sweet in nature and well-mannered. It was good for Holly to have some "normal" little girl playtime. Holly had enjoyed Cora's company in the past, so I was hopeful that the two of them would have innocent playtime.

As Donna and I sat down to a cup of freshly ground coffee, the girls went upstairs to play dress-up. Ann helped them get out the play jewelry and dress-up clothes while Donna and I stayed within earshot of the girls. About an hour into their play, Holly began to scream. I had heard that terror-filled, panicked scream when she triggered many times before. I bolted upstairs, scooped her up in my arms, and took her out of the room. Little Cora stood there wide-eyed and concerned.

"It's okay, honey, she will be okay." I reassured Cora as I carried a still-screaming Holly out of the room. Once in my room, I closed the door and held her.

"What is wrong, honey? Why are you screaming? What happened?"

"She is a scary!"

"Cora is a scary?"

"Yes, she has Naked Lady's hair! She was swinging her head and dancing, and her hair is like Naked Lady's!" she blurted out between gasping sobs.

"Honey, who is Naked Lady?"

"Grandpa's friend!"

"Grandpa's friend?"

"Yes!"

I reassured her, "I will tell Cora no more dancing. Cora is a nice little girl, not a scary. Cora just has dark hair, that is all. You are just *remembering* bad things, but the bad things are not happening now."

Holly still did not want to play anymore, so Ann kept Cora company while Holly stayed in my room. I assured Donna that Cora had done nothing wrong and that Holly just needed to rest, trying my best to keep from having to explain more. Donna took the hint that it was Holly's naptime. We wrapped up in the next half hour, and then she and Cora headed home. So much for the little girl playtime I had hoped for.

The triggering from Cora's dark hair had released another level of evil. From that day on, Holly began to draw pictures of Naked Lady almost daily. Naked Lady was always wearing what appeared to be underwear or nothing at all. Although the pictures were done in four-year-old artistry, they focused on areas of anatomy that gave her the name Naked Lady. Holly now hated anything related to ladies' underwear or lace: lingerie advertisements, her dress slip, ladies' sleepwear in the store, dresses with lace, and even doll clothes with lace. Everything she, her sisters, and I put on had to be lace-free, and no one could wear anything black.

Holly's disclosures about Naked Lady unfolded: "Grandma took me to Naked Lady's house and left me with Grandpa. Grandpa likes

Naked Lady. He was kissing her. I saw him. Naked Lady took my clothes off and made me wear yucky underwear clothes. Naked Lady lives in a dark-blue house. It has purple curtains in the bathroom. I saw other kids hurt at Naked Lady's house. Naked Lady has a boy called Satan she keeps in a cage. She has black, long hair. She gave me Gummy Worms so I'd stop crying. Grandma and Grandpa were there. I was hurt a "big time" and a "little time" at Naked Lady's and was poked with a pokie by Grandpa and Grandma. I saw a big girl like Ann get hurt. The people dressed funny at Naked Lady's and took yucky pictures."

As the details of this dark lady increased, Naked Lady became a frequent character in her disclosures as much as Bad Grandpa. At first, she was Grandpa's friend drawn with uncovered breasts and long hair, and then Holly would include herself in the pictures being harmed by this scantily-clad woman. Over a two-year process, Holly would tell us everything she remembered that happened with Grandpa and his "friends." Her disclosures were pieces of some of the same events, but in greater detail. Holly would describe the places she was taken and the evil abuse that occurred, and like a jigsaw puzzle, we saw how the pieces fit together as I saved all of her drawings and kept descriptive notes.

The "other children" Holly spoke of troubled me. Something needed to be done if other children were being harmed as well. Where was this house, who was this Naked Lady, and who were Grandpa's friends? I found myself looking for a deep-blue house within an easy driving distance of ours. I would purposely drive by any that seemed close in color to the one she described and watch in the rearview window for a reaction from the backseat, but there usually was none.

Then one day on the way back from Ann's violin lesson, Holly began to cry. "Go faster, Mom. I want to go home!" This was the second time she had reacted this way when passing through this area.

"Is something scaring you?"

"Yes, we just passed Naked Lady's house!"

In the months ahead, I would slow down and explore that area to look for a deep-blue-colored house, and there was one that sat up on the bluff. Holly had cringed back in her seat when we had passed it, but on another trip, she didn't seem to be bothered. I didn't know what to think. On my own, I had driven up the bluff and pulled in closer to get a better look and try to find out who lived there. Hanging in a small bathroom window were purple curtains that seemed to fit Holly's description. I wrote down the license plate numbers I saw on the cars parked in the street.

Our neighbor, Warren, was a municipal police officer, and his wife, Flora, was a social worker. Holly and their daughter, Abby, were playmates. They noticed how Holly would trigger and did not want to play with Abby if Warren was around. I had shared with them some of what had happened to Holly. Then one day Holly was going out for ice cream with Abby and Flora. On the way, she mentioned to Flora that a naked lady had hurt her. Flora took me aside when they returned and asked me more questions about what happened. With tears running down her cheeks, she offered their help in any way needed. Warren's jurisdiction was in a different county, so what help he could offer was limited, but he would run checks in judicial records on whatever he could access. He ran the plates on the cars and did research on the owner of the blue house, but no suspicious or criminal activity was recorded.

Holly often cringed around people at the grocery store. She would suddenly grab me, cry, and want to leave. There were similar characteristics in these people that frightened her. I would watch for the cars they would get in as they left the store, and at times, I would have Warren run their plates.

Holly refused to go to the local supermart, crying and begging me not to go there. For that reason, I no longer took her with me when I went. She said that one of Grandpa's friends lived close to the supermart and some of them shopped there. She spoke of a house nearby, and one day on a different outing in the same area she began to scream as we passed a green house. I had taken a wrong turn and was driving back around when we passed it. I had Warren check on it as well, but again, nothing of significance surfaced.

Warren informed me about the way pedophiles will take pornographic pictures of children and then meet at different locations to exchange them. The exchange of child porn is quite lucrative in the black market. It caused me to think back to her reaction during our recent family photo. She appeared frightened and asked if she had to take her clothes off. We had to assure her that no one would take their clothes off, and this was a studio and a nice place for family pictures. Holly spoke of small children being at both Naked Lady's house and Grandpa's friend's green house by the supermart. I needed to tell someone. As a concerned citizen, I felt I had to report her recent disclosures to the police.

CHAPTER 17 ～

REPORTING

IT HAD BEEN months since we had heard anything from the Victim Investigator's Office. Child Protection Services sent Holly's file to the DA, and we were told it would be a while until we heard back. We would have to walk through the slow legal process. They would be in contact with us when it was closer to time for my father's trial. If Holly made further disclosures to her counselor, we were to have Grace send a letter to the their office. Grace had mailed a letter, but we had not received a response. With concern for the other children Holly mentioned and a need for an update on her case, I placed a call to the Victim Investigator's Office. I never expected the response I received.

The Victim's investigating officer on the case abruptly cut me off as I began to tell her that my daughter informed me of places she had been taken where other children were harmed.

"I can understand how you may want to strengthen your daughter's case, but there is just no way that we can investigate this. Something like this may involve different counties; there is just no way."

I was stunned. *Strengthen my daughter's case? What was she implying?*

"Ma'am, I do not know what you mean about 'strengthening my daughter's case.' I am just informing you as a citizen that more children may be being harmed. What you do with that information is your responsibility as an officer of the law."

She mumbled something about passing on the information and ended the call. I had not been given an update, and I was too stunned to ask. I was puzzled and taken aback at the reprimand for my civilian concerns. Was this the advocate we were to work with, the person who would interact with us on our behalf with the DA? I felt insult had been added to injury. When I shared her response with Warren, he explained that unfortunately the smaller counties tended to prosecute cases that were neat and simple. It wasn't so much about protecting children as it was about time and budgets. Our case had just gotten more complicated.

After the call, I decided to avoid talking with our "advocate" in the future and would go directly to the DA's office. Later that month, I called his office, hoping the information had been passed on to him and to inquire about where they were in the process of pressing charges on behalf of Holly. He had already stated he would press charges against my father on behalf of Kristine and Diana, but he had not made a decision on Holly's case. Did they attach Holly's case to my nieces, or was it going to be filed separately? After playing phone tag for several days, I finally reached the DA and asked about the status of Holly's case.

"There really isn't much we can do about her case at this time. She has only stated that your father is a monster."

"What do you mean? Her counselor sent your office a letter more than a month ago reporting her disclosures. She has told her a great deal!"

"What letter? I never received a letter. Are you sure she sent one?"

"Yes, I have a copy of it here with me."

"Could you have her counselor resend us a copy of the letter? In the meantime, I will look into this."

"Yes, I will call her today."

"Can you tell me what she has disclosed?"

I told him everything that Holly had shared, even about Naked Lady. I explained how I attempted to inform the investigating officer of these things and that she had been uninterested because there was "no way" it could be followed up. He disagreed and felt that it may have been some of the missing pieces to the case and his office should look into the claims. He assured me that he would have a sit-down meeting with the officer regarding this matter and the missing letter. However, he was being reassigned to a different county and would be leaving the office by the end of the month. He would be advising the new DA on our case. I asked him to leave her file in competent hands.

The next day, the Victim's Advocate investigating officer that brushed me off earlier called with a very different demeanor. She was respectful and asked that I tell her everything Holly revealed. Then she tried to explain what she thought may have happened to the report from Grace.

I contacted Grace, and she sent another letter to the office. Hopefully, something would be done now that things appeared to be in better hands, at least for the time being. I had enough to deal with in helping Holly heal.

CHAPTER 18 ❧

THE BROKEN BABY

THE ANGER AND fear Holly felt was bigger than her small frame could handle. I held her one afternoon to calm and comfort her after another outburst. I had begun to see a pattern with these outbursts. When the triggering intensified, a flood of traumatic memories surfaced, and there were new disclosures and more details. Today was one of those wave-cresting days.

"God," I silently prayed as I held her, "what do I do?"

"Ask her about the baby."

Holly had commented months ago about a broken and burned baby. At the time, I didn't know how to respond. She had instantly changed her focus after she spoke of it, as if she had revealed all she could handle. What little she said had been hard enough on me as it was. Was I ready to hear more? Before I asked, Holly would need to feel very safe. I felt led to pray aloud for God to put us in a bubble, where the enemy could not hear or see us. Peace came upon Holly, and she quieted.

"Holly, can you tell me about a baby?"

She nodded, and with tears running down her face, she drew a picture, explaining as she went. "Grandpa took the skin off the baby. It cried, then it stopped. Grandpa put the baby in the fire."

Afterwards, I held her until her crying subsided. Then I asked the true Lord Jesus to speak to her about the baby.

She closed her eyes and spoke a few moments later. "Momma, Jesus has the baby. She is all better now." She looked relieved as she smiled up at me. It was the right time, and God knew Holly needed to share.

That evening, I put on her favorite Messianic worship CD. "Shalom, Shalom. Peace be with you ..." lullabied her to sleep.

Now, it was my turn to cry. "God, where were You? I prayed for her protection every night since she was a baby. Where were You?"

In a quiet peace I heard, *"She didn't fragment; I kept her."*

At the time, I didn't understand what a miracle it was that she had not been mentally shattered. She did not have multiple personality disorder (MPD)—a disorder that results in a fragmented personality with amnesic barriers due to severe trauma when very young. However, I understood why Job, spoken of in Scripture, sat in ashes and scraped himself with shattered pottery (Job 2). It wasn't just because he was opening boils, but the shattered pottery was a picture of his life. I felt like I was covered in ashes and that my childhood, protective mothering, and careful care of little Holly was now in pieces like broken pottery. Job had been innocent, and so were we. I wanted to smear ashes on my forehead and rub them on my clothes.

"God," I cried, "what kind of father kills babies? Why, why did this happen to Holly? Why couldn't I have known! Why didn't I know?"

"You are asking the wrong question. What you are struggling with is My sovereignty."

It wasn't the "why" that needed answering. It was my acknowledgement of His sovereignty and yielding to Him as Lord. It was the rest of the book of Job, not just the beginning. It was chapters 38–42 too.

CHAPTER 19 ❧

THE CHURCH

WHAT WE WERE facing isolated us because there was so much we couldn't express. It was as though I had to manage heaps of toxic waste. How much could I share without traumatizing the people who loved me? Just as I related to Job sitting in ashes, I also related to his being isolated in his pain while yet in the company of his friends.

I understood how Job's friends' worldview was rocked by his tragedy. My friends also couldn't grasp or relate to what I had to wrestle with. I understood why Job wanted to plead with God and how a person can be innocent, yet misunderstood. People don't understand how something so horrible could happen to the innocent. At times, people responded as if we had leprosy, as if what happened to us might infect them. They were suspicious and scrutinized us as if we were some kind of secretive, twisted family. When I did attempt to confide in a close friend about Holly seeing a baby killed, she cut me off quickly, saying, "Don't tell me anymore. I don't want to hear." So I didn't. I didn't tell anyone for a long time, except the counselor and Nick. It seemed I had to carry this without sharing it.

When I found the courage to share or explain Holly's behavior, I felt judged. People would ask questions, trying to determine why I hadn't known. I would have to educate them on how children continue functioning, how shame and fear keep them quiet, and how pedophiles can commit these crimes unnoticed. I was left feeling shamed and judged as a bad mother who somehow knew but was incompetent. It only added to the pain.

At times, I could handle people not knowing what to say, but it was the weeks of silence that was hardest. Our district pastor, who rarely called, acted as though the storm had passed when we were still in the midst of it. I knew he was a busy man; after all, our church had over five thousand members and only ten district pastors with a senior and assistant pastor. In the beginning, he called a couple of times to check on us and to pray with me. Now it was as though he thought all was well, and when we saw him at prayer meetings, he would not ask about our situation.

Like Job, I had to work through the pain from friends that said the wrong things or just couldn't handle our situation. Job sat silently and did not speak to his friends for seven days. Some pain is too deep to express because it is beyond the capacity of language. The pain I felt became a numbness, and I too stopped speaking. It was hidden until the late hours of the night. Then it came out in muffled moans and sobs as I lay on my closet floor.

I now understood why Nick's father, Papa, never talked about World War II until a few years before he died. He had unloaded the bodies of the Jews from the train cars in Germany and buried the remaining piles of bodies after the US troops invaded. This man who cherished family witnessed the devastation and carnage that remained of thousands of Jewish families. There were no words to describe what he had witnessed, and yet he had to return to the sheltered, Western world. This world didn't understand how a single man, Hitler, was capable of incredible depravity beyond what humanity wanted to accept. However, it is in the place of ignorance and denial where the darkest of evil hides.

While there were friends who avoided us, there were also faithful friends who *did something,* and that *something* made a difference … a huge difference. As much as I wanted to hide in a cave, those *somethings* pulled me back into the Christian community. Those who prayed for us were like jewels from heaven. Never in my life had the prayers of others meant so much. There was no way to put into words how much I valued prayer.

Irene was one of those friends who wasn't sure how to support us. However, when God burdened her, she responded and did *something* by not letting me pull away. When I tried to withdraw, she came after me and would not allow me to remain silent.

The Sunday following Holly's disclosure about the murdered baby, I walked into church numb and perplexed, with my eyes swollen from late-night tears. As I colored and played with paper dolls with Holly in the foyer, I tried my best to watch the service via the monitor screen that was set up in the reception area. Holly triggered from being around groups of people. She did not want to be in her Sunday school class or in the congregation. Without knowing what was going on, Irene came out from the service to find me in the foyer. God had burdened her heart to speak with me.

She said, "I think you are going to need to learn about some things you may not want to know about, but only enough to know how to deal with what you are dealing with. You don't want to get slimed."

She prayed for me to have wisdom, and as a peace came over me, the heaviness lifted. The message was the same one Edna had given me months ago, but this time, I knew I needed to study at a deeper level, as much as I didn't want to.

Then Irene pulled out a small vial of beautifully scented anointing oil. She had mixed essence of myrrh, frankincense, and a delicate rose and called it Holly's oil. She asked Holly if it would be okay if she prayed for her. Holly timidly said "yes," so Irene gently picked her up and placed her on her lap. She prayed for Holly and anointed her hands and forehead with the beautiful oil. Holly became peaceful as she sat with tears quietly slipping down her cheeks. Irene did not know what I had just faced with Holly, but God did, and He had sent Irene to minister to us.

Later in the week, my friend Becky felt burdened to give me a verse, so she wrote it out on pretty stationary. It was Isaiah 43:1–2, "Fear not, for I have redeemed you, I have called you by your name; you are Mine. When you pass through the waters, I will be with you." It was the same passage one of our district pastors had given us at the beginning of our journey.

CHAPTER 20 ❧

RITUAL ABUSE

I BEGAN TO spend more time researching on the Internet. I found sites for recovery, blogs for survivors, and sites discussing forms of ritual abuse. Some were written for survivors, and to my horror, some were written to instruct participants. The disclosures Holly made fit with some of the accounts I found by people who were victims of Satanic Ritual Abuse (SRA); only the abuse Holly suffered was not an ongoing experience but rather several isolated events.

My first exposure to the term "SRA" was at the Ellel training Nick and I had attended. An attendee at the school was recovering from SRA and suffered from a fear of snakes because they were used on her when she was abused. I had no idea what she meant by being an SRA survivor. I only noticed that she was accompanied by a counselor or psychologist and there appeared to be a level of protection around her.

I now found myself reading about types of ritual abuse purposely designed to control and silence the victims. This form of abuse is founded in a desire for power with a goal to destroy a person's moral values and personal identity. It uses different means of torture, horror, witnessing of violence, and forced participation in inhumane acts, and it requires victims to make double-bind choices where both result in the harm or death of another. The overall intent of SRA is to shatter and fragment a soul.

The preferred age for shattering with this type of abuse is infancy to age five. After age five, shattering becomes increasingly difficult. Severe trauma can cause a child to mentally escape unconsciously and disconnect psychologically from what is happening. This allows the child to go on functioning as though nothing happened … at least for a time.

A person can be raised in a cult or be secretly given to Satan in a ritual by an involved relative while the rest of the family is unaware. An individual can be lured into a cult for the promise of power, or a victim of various ages can be kidnapped for the use of torture, sacrifice, and the production of snuff films (pornography of the sickest form, where someone is killed). Young girls raised in cult families can be used to produce infants for sacrifices. These babies are taken early in gestation to avoid discovery. Kidnapped victims can be considered missing without drawing suspicion to a cult group. Evidence is burned and thoroughly disposed of, leaving no trace or trail.

Perpetrators involved in ritual abuse are experts at using terms for various acts that sound ridiculous when a child speaks them. They purposely attempt to give a child a false sense of reality. They will give different meanings to common terms and will dress in a variety of outfits to confuse or cause the child to remain unheard or believed.

For example, a child harmed by a person dressed like a bear (or in another costume) and forced to consume feces may say, "A big bear hurt me with his paw and made me eat yucky birthday cake."

Then mankind rationally assumes, "Hmm, sounds like a made-up story."

I had noticed I could no longer give Holly a time out for disobedience; it caused a huge trigger. She told me Grandpa put her in time outs. The innocent term "time out" meant something different now. Time out was being tied with a rope and put in a box, a circle of fire, or some type of a cage. "Naptime" was another trigger word. Naptime was when Grandpa would molest her and poke her. Many everyday terms I used now had completely different meanings to her. They were done intentionally to keep her in a state of fear and to make her disclosures appear insignificant or questionable. When these terms were used at home, she would become confused or fearful of those who loved her the most. Isolation from loved ones is a common tactic cultic group's use for control.

Cult groups network well with other similar groups. It is common for individuals in higher levels of secret societies to join hands with satanic priests in ritual ceremonies. All cult members do not always stroll around in black or don chains and body piercings. There are some who do, but those in the higher levels are encouraged to seek positions of respect in the community and to wear robes only in secret. Positions of respect and influence are often sought through leadership in churches, mission and civic organizations, law enforcement, and political offices. They strive to perfect a cover of light to operate behind in an effort to insure that any accusation ever made will not be believed.

I ordered books by some of the organizations that were helping victims of SRA. It took over a month for them to arrive, and when they finally did, there was a note from the sender. The books had been returned to the sender. Someone had intentionally ripped off the package label. The books were re-sent with the tampered packaging enclosed so that I could see the evidence of what had happened. It made me feel as though the more truth I uncovered, the more we were being watched. I began to battle a rising fear as I became increasingly aware of the type of people my father and his friends were.

I recalled that on the last day of Ellel training a few years earlier, God had clearly spoken to me. During one of the class breaks, I was standing outside on the balcony admiring the view of the meadow when He spoke.

"The biggest battle you will ever face will be against your father."

At the time, I had no idea what the Lord meant; yet His words were so clear. I didn't understand then why He told me this, but now those words echoed in my thoughts and gripped my heart.

As I learned more about various types of ritual abuse, it was as if God was preparing me for the next wave of what Holly would share. Holly spoke of ladies in purple or green robes and of being put in the middle of a circle of fire. She mentioned the hat my dad wore and would draw pictures of it frequently. It wasn't a witch's hat, but it was similar to a wizard's or druid's. When we were shopping, she would see fabrics or colors that would remind her of what Grandpa and his friends would wear during rituals. She would feel panicked and start shutting down by whimpering, cringing, and cowering.

Now Holly regularly triggered over staining her clothes, spilling water on herself, getting dressed or undressed, taking a bath, candles, fire, the color black, and the color dark blue. She refused to eat certain foods—foods that used to be her favorites at one time. Now their color or texture bothered her. It was increasingly difficult to find things she would willingly eat. Then one evening she started triggering over a peanut butter and jelly sandwich, of all things.

While preparing for bed, she started yelling in her room. "I don't care anymore! I don't care about people!" She was yelling and crying so I went and held her, and she said, "But I do care, Mom."

"I know."

Then she cried harder, "I hate peanut butter and jelly. I hate it!"

With a pen and paper, she drew a picture and told me why she hated it. Peanut butter was the color of feces she was forced to eat with jelly.

Holly also talked about hot blood that was put on her neck by Grandpa and a "wipey" that was used to wipe it off. She spoke of people with blood on their fingers and of them drinking something foul from a goblet. She talked about saws, swords, and knives used to cut and dismember victims and that Grandpa had guns he threatened to use. In Play Therapy, she would often depict Grandpa as the paper doll in the witch costume or as the Grim Reaper figure. She would talk about being tied up, and she hated having anything around her waist. She would refuse to wear belts, decorative ties, or anything else that reminded her of a rope. She would tug at her pants until they were below her waist and slipping off her hips.

She also said she saw monsters and scaries that would threaten her when she told me details about the rituals. Her lips would begin to feel hot and sometimes would swell to twice their size, causing her to holler in pain. It was apparent that her body had memory and reacted to the things she recalled. I would learn that memories could be fragmented from our awareness and surface in bodily responses through triggering. When her lips felt hot and swelled, I would pray and anoint them with her special oil. Peace would come over Holly, her lips would stop hurting, and then they would return to normal.

She explained to me that something hot was put on her lips by Grandpa, like a fire that didn't burn. I could only assume he somehow created a burning sensation on her lips to threaten her not to talk. I later discovered, via the Internet, that there is an ointment used to give horrific burning sensations without physically causing any burns or irritations.

There were times I could feel a dark presence in the room tormenting her. It would leave during our prayers. I anointed the windows and doors of our house, asking God to seal them from the attempts of the enemy entering, tormenting, or seeing us.

Following the baby disclosure, I now regularly prayed for Jesus to place a bubble around her so she would feel safe enough to talk and so the demonic would not harass her. Afterwards, she would no longer hear threatening voices or feel pain. She would calm down enough to draw, releasing the trauma until its intensity would subside. The tangible presence of the Lord was a shelter and gave us both a sense of safety.

CHAPTER 21 ❧

MIRACLES

ONE AFTERNOON WHILE we were rocking, she began to feel fearful when I said the name "Jesus." I did not understand why she suddenly felt afraid of Jesus' name. Not only had I prayed this way with her many times before, but also we had taught her that Jesus loves children very much. She started yelling and screaming in a panic for me not to pray to Jesus.

Lord, I silently prayed, *what is this? What should I do?*

"Ask her about a bad Jesus."

Bad Jesus? I questioned. "Holly, can you tell me about Bad Jesus"?

Instantly, she was terrified and began to yell even louder, saying, "I can't talk about it! I can't talk about it!"

In response, I asked the Lord to put us in His bubble, but she kept yelling while looking over at the corner of the room.

"Holly, what do you see?"

"Bad Jesus!" she hollered, and she pointed to the corner of the room.

I knew we were dealing with something demonic that was threatening her.

"Holly, would you like to have the true Lord Jesus, who loves children and never hurts them, make the Bad Jesus leave?"

"Yes, Mommy, yes!"

So I prayed, "True Lord Jesus, can you come and show Holly how you are stronger than the scaries and this Bad Jesus? Can you make him leave?"

Before I had gotten to "amen," Holly started laughing. "Mommy, the true Jesus has a sword, and when the Bad Jesus saw it, he went running out of the room!"

Holly never saw Bad Jesus again. Whatever had been tormenting her was gone. From then on, she was no longer fearful when sharing, no longer needed oil for her lips, and no longer passed out. Peace was taking the place of the fear. She had seen with her own eyes that the true Lord Jesus was bigger than anything she was facing.

Another amazing miracle happened on the day she realized that her eldest brother, Joseph, was not a scary. I found Joseph slumped over the kitchen counter, sobbing from a flood of emotions he could no longer contain.

"What's wrong, Joseph? What's happened?"

He managed to blubber out, "Holly just came in my room and asked to sit on my lap."

Choking up again, he paused to regain composure and continued, "Do you know what she said, Mom? She told me, 'Joseph, you're not a scary. You're a nice brother, a nice guy. You're not a monster.'"

Then he broke down, and I held him in my arms. This was the little sister he nicknamed "Peaches" from the first day he held her at the hospital. This was the same girl he was so protective of, who tackled him when he came home from school and who loved to tease and tickle him. This was the little girl who had Joseph's heart wrapped around her pinky. Overnight he had become a scary, simply because he was a man. For months he had to ask just to hug her. He could not tickle or play with her, and he had to approach her cautiously and speak softly to her.

Today she asked to be held, and it took him by surprise. He carefully lifted her up and gently put his arms around her. For a while, she just sat with him as he choked back the tears, and then she got down. Joseph, overcome by emotion, had come downstairs so she wouldn't know he was crying. We both knew he had just experienced a miracle in her journey of healing, and there would be more to come. The abuse had made Holly view all men as "monsters," even the ones who would have given their lives if necessary to protect her. This was the day she realized that there are safe men after all. A moment of healing had taken place for her and Joseph. From that moment, Holly began to see how safe and protective the men around her actually were. It really was a miracle.

CHAPTER 22 ❧

LOOKING BACK AND GOING FORWARD

HOLLY FELT SAFE talking with her counselor, Grace. "Grandpa doesn't know Grace. He doesn't know about her," she would say confidently.

While I had struggled to come to terms with the horrible things Holly was disclosing, Grace was struggling to accept the reality of what she was hearing. She often questioned if Holly's experiences were from a spiritual dimension, similar to nightmares. While she knew that some of the events happened in the physical, when it came to Holly talking about a baby being burned, Grace preferred to see it as a spiritual experience. True, it would have been easier to accept it as a non-physical experience. However, I knew we were dealing with actual events that had spiritual components. They were not merely a nightmare.

I could tell when Holly was talking of the scaries in her sleep or in the room versus the scaries that were Grandpa's friends who wore strange clothes. The scaries in her sleep looked like scribbles with angry eyes and blobbed forms on paper. The scaries that were Grandpa's friends had bodies, wore hats, and Holly was surrounded by them while being abused. Her drawings were consistently the same.

Holly had talked about scaries, and she had talked about angels too. She told me that when Grandpa, Naked Lady, and Grandpa's friends were hurting her, she cried out for me, and an angel came and brought her to me. All I could assume was that she had disassociated into the Lord's presence, and He had kept her until I had picked her up at Grandma's.

While I agreed with Grace that Holly had some experiences in the spiritual realm (like Bad Jesus), I also knew that many of the things she experienced were real events. Grace had been a great help to Holly, but we had come to a place in Holly's therapy that was out of Grace's comfort zone and experience base. Grace had hoped she would get a better picture from counseling Travis's girls to compare events, but they never attended consistently and quit shortly after the Play Therapy training. I began to look for someone who was more skilled and experienced for Holly and me.

It is said hindsight is 20/20. If we only knew then what we know *now*. I was living with the turmoil of the "if only" that was tearing at me. If only I had noticed how groggy Holly was from "naps" after I would pick her up. I *now* remembered there were times she would fuss and want to leave right away, but I figured she was tired since her nap had been interrupted. I requested that Mom try to keep her up and not put her down for naps so I could put her down for one at home. Mom would tell me that she fell asleep when she read her stories, but now I wondered if her "naps" were a dose of Benadryl or something else. Holly mentioned being given "yucky medicine" and would throw fits anytime she ran a fever and had to take liquid Tylenol.

Now I remembered when she was two or three there were times her vaginal area would be red and itchy, so I would put medicated cream on it. It would come and go, but I thought it was because she was learning to wipe herself and had irritated the area.

I *now* remembered our younger son, Timothy, telling me that Grandpa was holding Holly in the living room and he suddenly heard her yell. Grandpa told him she was fine and to continue playing on the computer. It had upset him, and he told me on the way home from Grandpa's. He did not know what had made her yell. Timothy had occasionally stayed at my parents as well, but less often. He was old enough to attend some of the co-op classes for the younger students when they were offered.

Now I remembered the day I was teaching at the co-op and Dad was supposed to bring Holly to me after my class. When he didn't show, I called Mom, and she said he had to run errands uptown first. I waited and waited and could not understand what was taking so long. I actually started to feel panicked, but I didn't know why. It was as though the Lord was stirring my heart.

When my dad finally arrived, Holly was groggy, and he laid her down on a mat to sleep. I remember it bothered me so much that he seemed to take forever, but he gave no explanation for the delay. All he said was that he had made a few stops. I felt uneasy leaving her with Mom and Dad, so I made excuses and told Mom I didn't need her to watch Holly when I taught. Holly was getting old enough to come with me.

I didn't have a reason for feeling troubled, only an irrational panic that didn't make sense. I felt concerned about her care, as though something bad was happening. I had no frame of reference in my mind and no reason for my concern, only this stirring in my heart that was contrary to rational thought. It seemed that the Lord was troubling my heart about leaving her with my parents, and I was beginning to hear His warnings and tune into His voice in a clearer way. I *now* remembered, and it goaded me in the night when I tried to sleep. *Now* I wondered why I had doubted the unease in my spirit.

As a young child, I was often told by my parents that I was oversensitive, made a big deal out of nothing, and was too serious. I would often sense things and be laughed at by others or be belittled by my father for being a bit of a Pollyanna. (That's what he would call me.) At a young age, I stopped paying attention to the stirrings of my heart as best I could, or I pushed real hard inside until that sensitivity was buried deep. In the past year, I felt the Lord begin to heal me and help me to accept myself for the way He made me. I was beginning to "sense" more again, but the words my parents had spoken when I was small still scolded in my thoughts and created a conflict. I doubted what I sensed was as reliable as what I could see. I needed a place to sort out the inner conflict and to wrestle through all the "if only" thoughts and come to a place of peace.

Through a referral, I made an appointment with Fay Johnson. She had worked with ritual survivors, worked as a social worker, and had a strong experience base as a counselor with trauma and post-traumatic stress. Her office became my haven. Because she was a professional and I paid for her time, I felt less inclined to hold back from dumping the horror of what we were facing as a family. Although she felt like a close friend, she was a professional I had hired. This is what she was paid to do. I did not need to protect her or our friendship, and I did not need to manage the amount of toxic waste I unloaded in her office.

Her truthful responses and strong faith strengthened me, and I would come in overwhelmed and leave with courage. She was familiar with the things I was telling her, and it didn't shock her as it had shocked me. I felt validated and believed. She didn't pull away like I had leprosy. Instead, she helped me to understand why it felt like the church had abandoned us. She gave me resources and connections to incredible ministries. I ordered exceptional books by James Wilder: *Red Dragon Cast Down, The Life Model,* and others. I purchased comforting materials by Arthur Burke and attended training seminars by Tom Hawkins with Restoration in Christ Ministries. I had found a place of solace and comfort, as well as an arsenal for spiritual battle. God had allowed the bad to happen to us, but He had called in the cavalry. Sinful men and women had made evil choices, but God had a restoration plan in motion and was giving me keys to unlock "hidden treasure in dark places" (Isaiah 45:3). I read and devoured these amazing resources as though they were food rations in a third-world country.

CHAPTER 23 ❧

BROTHERS IN DENIAL

MY ELDEST BROTHER, Wendell, lived out of state, and Travis felt it was time for him to know what had happened. Wendell was wrapped up in his political career. He had served as the city mayor and had been the campaign manager for several important legislative offices. The people he promoted, won. He was skilled at what he did and sought to land a position of power and influence in the political arena. Having parents of notable state involvement had been a great advantage for him. He was divorced, and his children were grown and beginning to establish their own lives.

When Travis told Wendell about his daughters' abuse, Wendell questioned Travis about whether or not he was sure. Travis told him he was, but Wendell seemed unconcerned and brushed Travis off. Travis was angry and perplexed at Wendell's response and called me to vent.

Ellen had been calling as well to share her struggles with Kristine and update me on anything she heard from the DA's office. Kristine was behaving horribly. She was lighting things on fire, having screaming fits, reacting extremely fearfully, refusing to sleep alone, acting aggressive, and stealing things. She was repeatedly missing school and flunking most of her classes. Due to Kristine's behavior, the CPS required Travis and

Ellen to attend classes dealing with sexual abuse to help improve their parenting of Kristine.

Travis completed only two of the classes. On the way home from the second class, he pulled his car over to a curb and sat on the side of the road, sobbing. Then he repeatedly tried to throw himself in front of oncoming traffic while Ellen screamed and attempted to restrain him. Nick and I thought the timing seemed right to meet with them and share what we had learned from Holly's disclosures, in hopes that it would help them with Kristine. We also needed to get a better understanding of how Travis was functioning. Perhaps it might help them uncover what was causing Kristine's fixations with fire and her heightened, excessive fears. Travis also needed to know how unsafe Mom was and the importance of completely breaking his unhealthy connection with her.

Nick and I drove over to their house after supper. Ellen greeted us, and we made ourselves comfortable on the sofa. She jokingly commented on how I could actually sit on the sofa, now that she had finished folding the pile of laundry that had been there.

"Bet you wondered if we had one under all of that," she said.

I told her how nice the house looked. It was cleaner than it was the last time I had seen it. I could tell they had tried to assemble a bit more order for our arrival or for the regular Child Protection Service evaluations. They were receiving food stamps, so the children were eating well, and Ellen, who was pregnant with their fifth child, appeared healthier. After we hugged and greeted the children, Travis told Kristine to take the younger ones outside while we talked.

I shared with Travis some of the strange things Holly was disclosing and asked if he had heard anything similar from Kristine. He replied that Kristine was so full of fear that she was not telling them much. They had purchased alarms for the windows, and all the children were constantly sleeping with Travis and Ellen on the floor in their bedroom.

Then Travis shrugged and laughed nervously. "Heck, it wouldn't surprise me if bodies started appearing. You know, I have thought about digging around the sand bar near the house they used to live in by the river, just to see if I could find something." He went on and talked of how strangely quiet Wendell was being and how it bugged him.

When the children came back inside, they began quarreling, so we took the hint and said our good-byes. Travis indicated that he was not ready to sever his ties with Mom, and he once again seemed unconcerned about Kristine's pain. He either couldn't deal with it or refused to come out of denial.

CHAPTER 24 ❧

CLEANSING AND RECOVERY

WITH ALL THE material I was reading, as well as the drawings and disclosures Holly was making, I felt strongly impressed by the Lord that the rituals performed had spiritual dimensions that needed cleansing. Some of these rituals involved mock marriages to Satan or to the abuser as a form of control.

After playing "married" earlier in her room, Holly told her sister that Grandpa played married with her.

Ann had questioned Holly, "Did he play married with dolls?"

"No, just me and him; he had something sticking out of his pants, and it hurt me by my potty part."

Ann waited until Holly was occupied before coming to me upset. She handed me the scrap of paper, where she had written down what Holly had said. Holly's strange fixation on playing married was by itself enough of a clue. We prayed and broke any vow she was forced into based on the passage in Numbers 30, where a father, once aware of a vow that his daughter had spoken, could nullify that vow. We asked the Lord to sever any connection between Holly and Grandpa related to the sexual abuse and marriage rituals.

I then had Holly take a bath in my bathtub. It was a garden tub, which was a special treat to bathe in. I took some of Holly's oil and added it to the water. Then I prayed and ask Jesus to wash Holly in the physical and in the spiritual as she bathed. I asked Him to sanctify the water, just as water was set aside for cleansings in the temple.

Holly got in, and it was unlike any bath she had ever taken. She entered into the water without fear, surrounded by an amazing peace. When she was done, she was restful and told me that the bad water, hot blood, "yukies" from Grandpa, and "poopies" were all gone. She felt clean throughout her body and in her heart.

God spoke to me a few days after her special bath. *"If you have her dedicated at church, it will undo the ritual dedication."*

I called our district pastor and asked if he could arrange a private dedication since Holly was unable to be in front of crowds of people. He agreed to talk with the senior pastor and would let me know what could be scheduled.

In the meantime, Holly began to destroy things. I would find her dolls headless in her room, dumped trash cans from the bathroom, shredded papers strewn about, or a broken glass on the floor. When I would question her about what happened or who made the mess, she would tell me it wasn't her but it was the "bad girl." Then she would fall apart crying if I pressed her further. One day after she came out of her room, I walked in a few minutes later to find a book torn apart. She denied destroying it, but it was obvious she had because no one else had been in the room.

When I questioned her further, she cried and yelled back, "Mommy, I didn't do it! It was the bad girl! I told you. She did it! She keeps doing bad things!"

At that moment, I recognized that Holly was trying to see herself in two parts: the part that did the bad things and the part that was an innocent victim.

During my next visit with my counselor, Fay, I told her about Holly's recent episodes and the anger she was expressing through this "bad girl" behavior. Fay believed that what Holly had been disclosing were real events, so I asked if she would be willing to meet with Holly since we were in the process of finding a new counselor for her. As a rule, she did not work with children and felt uneasy. She agreed to meet with Holly if I was also in the session and would help her put things on Holly's level. I gave her suggestions for Play Therapy toys that might be helpful for the session and scheduled an appointment.

On the way to our meeting, I told Holly that Fay was someone else Grandpa didn't know, and she was my safe friend that we were going to visit. Holly was a little uneasy at first, until Fay began to play with her on the floor with the Play Therapy toys.

The first hour was a trust-building play time, and then Fay began to talk about the bad girl that was getting Holly in trouble. Fay prayed and instructed Holly to listen for Jesus to speak to her. When Fay prayed or asked a question, I would repeat it to Holly on a four-year-old's level.

Toward the end of the two-hour session, Holly admitted that the bad girl was not someone else but a part of her. She didn't like her because of what she had done. Holly shared with Fay that the bad girl had to poke a baby girl before Grandpa killed the baby and put her in the fire. She also had to poke a big girl like Ann in the stomach with a needle, but the big girl knew that Holly didn't want to do it. Holly saw the look in her eyes and could tell she understood that Holly didn't want to hurt her. The big girl cried and wanted her mommy too. Holly cried while Fay and I did our best to hold back our own sorrow.

Holly then forgave herself (the bad girl) and recognized that she wasn't bad; she was just forced to do bad things. She understood she was a good girl and that was why she didn't want to do the bad things Grandpa made her do. She was the same girl. All of her was loved by the true Lord Jesus, and He wanted her to love all of herself as well. It was as though there was this team of three: Jesus directing the session, Fay following His lead, and me coming along to help Holly understand.

At the end of the appointment, Fay had Holly sit with her older brother in the waiting area while she spoke with me privately.

"Do you realize what a miracle it is that Holly does not have multiple personality disorder—that she is not fragmented?" She spoke of how Holly remembered detailed events, and it was obvious Holly knew what she was talking about. Children who endure what Holly had faced typically end up with multiple personality disorder, also known as dissociative identity disorder (DID). Holly had only one division within her, and it was not from an amnesic barrier but from a barrier of self-rejection.

Holly's behavior was no longer destructive. In the future, she would tear paper or destroy toys only with permission in therapy. We had witnessed another miracle of healing in Holly. Fay had discovered that working with a child was similar to working with isolated child-like personality fragments in a shattered adult. I heard God's answer to my question of "Where were You?" echoed again. He had kept Holly from shattering, even though I still had not fully realized what an amazing miracle it was.

Holly's recent disclosures were revealing how the trauma was purposely devised to isolate her from those she loved and rebind her to the abuser. They told her that I had left her with my dad so he could hurt her and that I knew what my father was doing. They said I was a bad mom and she needed new parents. My dad introduced her to a scantily clothed couple with dark complexions during a ritual and said they were her "new parents." He told Holly he would kill me and burn our house down if she told. It was her fault the baby was hurt, and if she told on him and his friends, they would hurt her more.

The confusion laid down would sometimes surface during our prayer time, and she would suddenly look at me surprised and ask, "You're my mommy, right?"

I assured her that I had always been her mommy, and I had carried her inside me like I did her baby sister. A rational-minded adult would never believe the lies they had staged, but to a child of three or four, it was a different story.

As she progressively realized how Grandpa had lied to her about everything, she became enraged and would destroy the toys used to represent him in Play Therapy. She would scribble over drawings of him and instruct to me draw a jail cell around him. She would punch her pillow and jump on the trampoline, yelling out her anger as though he were listening.

While she seemed to be moving from overwhelming fear to an intense anger, I was struggling with a mounting, hidden torment. Nothing could hurt me more as a mother than to know I was not there when my child suffered, my child had felt abandoned, and was told she was purposely left so she could be harmed. Holly had carried that torment for months, and I had not known. The pain I felt was beyond words. I felt like someone who had come from the horrors of a concentration camp. I no longer knew how to relate to people in the church, people who could laugh and be silly or connect with close friends. The ash pile of Job was the only place I felt at home; yet I needed to reconnect with others, and I just didn't know how. I needed to find a way back to a place of joy again, but it seemed like a mirage on a distant desert horizon that moved farther away each time I tried to approach it.

CHAPTER 25 ❧

THE SHAWL

A BOX ARRIVED in the mail that had been sent by Vivian, a dear friend from the Great Lakes area. Inside was the softest of angora yarn crocheted into a beautiful, fringed shawl. There was a thickness to the yarn, but it was plush and felt like cotton puffs.

There was also a letter enclosed that read:

> This prayer shawl is for you. It was knit by my hands, and it was made with love and prayers. With nearly each turn of the needle, you were remembered and lifted in prayer. At other times, I was struggling with my own human errors. Should you find any mistakes that I couldn't see, may they remind you of our imperfections; yet God sees the overall, beautiful picture and loves us as He loves His only Son. He makes us perfect and blameless in Him. My hope is that this shawl will bring you some warmth and comfort as you wear it in prayer and that you may feel the presence of the Lord wrapping His loving arms around you and the love of your many friends. I pray that God's love and strength will shelter you and bring you His comfort, peace, and wisdom and give you the desires of your heart. With love and gratitude for the richness you've brought into my life, Vivian.

I sat and wept. I had returned the quilt my earthly mother had made, but now God was giving me a new heirloom. I had a different inheritance. I had given up "father ... mother ... [and] lands" (Matt. 19:29), but God had given me a friend who ministered to my heart as a mother would. She had taken the shawl to church before she mailed it, and had others gather and pray over the shawl, carefully anointing it. The sweet smell enveloped me as I wrapped myself in the soft yarn, and it soon found its place on my rocking chair. Holly and I would wrap ourselves in it during our rockie times. I would remember that even though I felt isolated in this valley, there were precious friends who loved me and were praying for us.

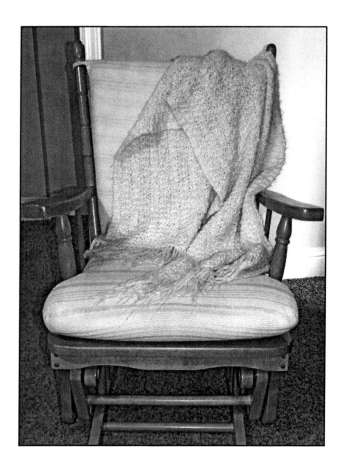

CHAPTER 26 ∾

HIDDEN EVIL AND THOSE WOUNDED

VIVIAN'S GIFT AND the reminder of praying friends gave me encouragement—a place of love where I could reflect while I came to terms with the evil that had assaulted our family and the loss of a childhood I once thought was true. I had to face the reality of a hidden, evil world that continued to harm children every day. I had to expose its methods of harm.

Its victims bear the labels of different mental disorders: bipolar, obsessive compulsive, false memory syndrome, schizophrenia, dissociative identity disorder (DID), etc. It is easier and more convenient for people to place a label on someone who speaks of ritual abuse rather than wrestle with the truth of its existence. Some victims are in families of satanic cults where ritual abuse continues from one generation to the next, and some are Lucifinerian. They refer to Satan as Lucifer and see him as the morning star revealed in the upper levels of Masonry. They go to great lengths to develop and perfect a covering of light. They create counteractions that oppose their dark, secretive efforts in order to strengthen the innocent façade. It is in this contrast that the truth is hidden. They strive to ascend into light so that they may descend into darkness.

They also are skilled in evil, abusive practices that accomplish severe damage in brief periods of time. Not all who are skilled in these dark techniques profess to believe in a devil; rather, their goal is to manipulate and control others for power, money, and political gain. All of them are part of an Antichrist agenda designed to destroy the next generation of children so that they may be used for dirty deeds or to prevent them from fulfilling their God-given destiny.

When these shattered victims find enough courage to talk, those in this evil use their positions in leadership and legislative connections to silence them. They will use court cases that never come to fruition, death threats, retaliation, or "false memory" accusations.

The caution I received from the CPS (about discussing Holly's abuse) regarding the possible implantation of false memory was a mystery to me until I realized the root of this misnomer. I had never heard of such a term and found it strange. I began to research its origins. I thought perhaps it could be associated with a form of hypnosis. I discovered that false memory syndrome was created by Peter Freyd, a mathematician, who coined the term after his daughter, a professor of psychology, accused him of sexually abusing her. He went on to establish the False Memory Syndrome Foundation that has had some influential board members of suspicious backgrounds. They use their status to promote the concept that relationships and self-identity can be affected by fabricated or incorrect memories. In my opinion, it appeared to be a form of denial in a palatable appearance. Accusing a victim of "false memory" can help restore a prominent offender's public image and conceal a lucrative network's operation from investigation.

Although the "false memory" term is well-known and made to appear as a mental condition, it is not officially classified by professional guidelines as a mental disorder. However, it is a convenient ploy to promote this concept for those involved in an evil, Antichrist mind-control agenda.

With the use of false memory allegations, victims are made to appear as perpetrators against the accused, while pedophiles and cultists appear as innocent martyrs. I now consider those quickest to silence or label victims with false memory as suspect or misinformed. Regardless of degrees or Christian standing, I question the "why" and roots of anyone's attempt to discredit those severely mistreated.

Some victims will turn to the church for support, but like the Pharisees who passed the beaten man on the road, the church may feel it is too messy or is unaware of the depths of evil. Some will question or label the victim in disbelief and are unsure how to help, so they do nothing. Yet, not knowing what to do can be the first step toward leaning on the One who does know. When God brings such broken, precious people to a congregation or pastor, there is an opportunity for that church to lay aside preconceived notions and religious programs and release the Holy Spirit to lead them in healing.

I once attended a Sunday service where the pastor claimed people who heard voices in their heads or felt they had separate parts to their personality were hearing demons. It wasn't an issue of a multiple personality disorder; it was a mindset, and the enemy needed to be rebuked. I cringed inside. What if someone in the audience had MPD and needed a safe place to heal? The church would not feel safe to that person after that statement. The pastor spoke out of ignorance, but as a leader, he was esteemed as knowledgeable and in a position that can so easily edify or injure.

At another service in a different church, the pastor shared with some members about a lady who visited his church and had come forward for prayer. He said she spoke about being the victim of SRA. He had the prayer team take her aside for a prayer session and then ended the prayer after thirty minutes so he could lock up the church and go to lunch. He behaved as though she suffered from mental issues and distanced himself from helping her any further. I thought of her brokenness and how she mustered the courage to speak of the harm she had faced but was brushed off as a "mental case."

The frightening fact is that ritual abuse and its consequential fruit of shattered victims is prevalent and increasing. Movies like the *Manchurian Candidate* and *Bourne Identity* have an element of reality that most people don't realize. Instead of the real-life victims being adults, they are usually small children. While some people who are recovering from such severe abuse have obsessive behaviors, depression, instability, paranoia, and panic attacks, they are neither insane nor delusional. They are shell-shocked and in need of a safe place with a loving community in which to heal. The church *should* be this type of community. Jesus did not injure a bruised reed, and He cautioned us about our treatment of what we see as the least of these (Matt. 25:37–40). I struggled with forgiving myself and the church for what we did not know. Yet, the same community I was struggling with was the one I had to connect with for healing.

CHAPTER 27 ❧

THE EXAM

NOW THAT WE had a better picture of the things that had happened to Holly, I had a greater concern for her physical well-being. She needed a blood panel run for HIV and any hidden STDs. Even though she no longer showed signs of any irritations, I wanted her examined internally. Her disclosures of pokies, needles, and occasional painful bowel movements caused me to be concerned that something could possibly still be inside her. I set up an appointment with a pediatrician, who then referred us to a pediatric surgeon since Holly would need to be under anesthesia for the exam. It would be traumatizing for her any other way.

Dr. Gareth was an attractive, middle-aged woman with a child of her own. She was gentle with both of us, and Holly felt safe talking to her. She asked Holly if she knew why she had come to the see her.

"Yes, cause Grandpa poked me, and you are going to see if my owies are all better."

She smiled at Holly and told her she was right.

A few weeks later, Holly was admitted into the pediatric ward of the hospital. She made it through her IV, which was hard on her. Thankfully, it was over quickly, as the nurse was experienced and had taken time to numb her skin. Holly became drowsy from the IV drip while watching cartoons. Once she was asleep, they wheeled her into the surgery room.

Her admitting nurse invited me to watch the exam from the nurses' station via their monitoring system.

The nurses were tender towards me. They were moms too. Their children's pictures were taped to the sides of computer screens and set on desk tops in various frames. I cried as I watched Holly's legs spread with her feet put in stirrups. I was having my daughter tested and examined for STDs, AIDS, and vaginal and rectal injury, and she was barely five.

Holly thrashed and panicked as she came out of the anesthetic. I held her down from one side of the bed, and two nurses steadied her on the other. They gave her a sedative and gradually brought her back to consciousness. It had been a long day.

The doctor said that she had found no vaginal damage, but the rectum had fissures that were not the type associated with constipation. They were indicative of trauma, especially because of the location. Her report read: "Atypical locations of fissures are suggestive of perianal trauma and may be consistent with sexual abuse." We never saw anything because they were located up high. Holly was to have Sitz baths every day and stay on a mild fiber drink until the fissures healed. Since it had been over a year since she was harmed, I asked Dr. Gareth why Holly still had them.

"They take that long to heal," she said.

She told me she would be sending a report with her findings to the DA. All of Holly's blood tests came back normal, and I found myself profoundly grateful that all the things that might have happened didn't.

C H A P T E R   2 8

A NEW THERAPIST

HOLLY BEGAN TO see Dr. Vera Howell to whom Fay had referred us. We had been looking for someone more skilled than Grace, and Dr. Vera had actually been one of Grace's professors in college.

Dr. Vera had worked with the FBI when she lived in the Midwest and saw things that never reached the news. She knew that on certain satanic holidays there would be a call from the FBI because they had found a body, or sometimes parts of a body, directly related to the ritualistic holidays. Professional therapy was needed for the notified family or the involved officers. It was common knowledge among the police force that someone would go missing on Halloween. The FBI and local police kept this quiet in order to prevent panic in the community.

When Holly began to tell Vera about the murdered baby, Vera believed her. Holly began to process memories and pain more rapidly with her new therapist. Vera suggested we buy a cuddly toy that would help Holly stay connected to the present. When Holly triggered, she could hold the toy and know that she was in "now time" and was only remembering. I bought her a stuffed lamb that she named "Lammy." Whenever traumatic memories surfaced and caused her to scream or cry, we would grab Lammy to calm her. Lammy went everywhere with Holly.

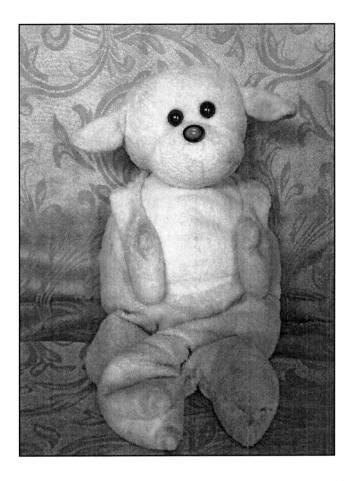

Vera had three therapy dogs and a cat she had rescued. The dogs had been neglected, and because one was severely abused, it was very timid. The dogs were very gentle, submissive, and seemed to be especially sensitive to emotional pain in people. Holly loved to snuggle next to them during her sessions. They made her feel protected and comforted.

Vera used sand tray therapy, in which figures were set up in a small sand box to express Holly's emotions. She would have Holly make "her" world. At first, Holly's world was full of angel figurines, wooden walls, and rock boundaries to protect her from the evil figures she positioned on the other side. Over time, there were fewer evil figures and fewer walls. As she healed, more beautiful things were added to her sand-tray world. Vera would have me sit in during some of these sand-tray sessions.

Between her appointments, I would duplicate the techniques I saw Vera use with Holly by using a small sand box at home.

Vera would confer with me on how Holly was doing, making suggestions or getting my input. During one of Holly's appointments, she had Holly play in the other room for part of the session while we talked. She assured me that if her case was brought to trial, she would testify as a professional on Holly's behalf as to the legitimacy of her memories.

She said, "Holly knows what she's talking about. She's not making this up, and you need to know that it's a miracle she's not multiple and that she has done so well."

I was reminded again of the Lord's words to me: *"I kept her. She did not fragment."*

CHAPTER 29 ❦

A RECONNECTING

THE CHURCH OFFICE called us back about our earlier request for a private dedication for Holly. A date was finally set when the senior pastor would be available. We were to meet him between services. As the senior pastor of a church with five thousand members on four campuses and who was also a noted author, speaker, and busy father, reserving time with him had been a challenge.

We met with him privately in the church conference room. He gently bent down, shook Holly's hand, and greeted her. Then he asked if he could hold her, and Holly timidly nodded her head. Pastor lifted her up in his arms and prayed a beautiful dedication over her. Holly wrapped her arms around his neck and hugged him tightly. His eyes pooled with tears. He put her down, then prayed over our family and gave Holly a small, pink Bible with the date recorded on the inside cover.

Holly had known who Pastor was because she watched him preach each Sunday on the monitor screen in the foyer. Before her dedication, he was just another man in a crowded room. Now she had made a personal connection, and he was her kind pastor who told lots of people about the true Lord Jesus. In the Sundays to come, she wanted to sit in the back of the church instead of the foyer so she could see him. At the end of the services, she would seek him out to give him a hug. Holly was slowly overcoming her fear of crowds by connecting to the church

103

community. Our tenderhearted senior pastor was used by God as a vessel of restoration more than he realized.

Our district pastor had not known how to handle what we were going through and had done little as a result. However, he became the catalyst for healing that I needed to reconnect to the church.

It was Mother's Day, and the district pastors and our senior pastor had selected three mothers they wanted to give special recognition to. One mother was a leader within the church who ministered to struggling married couples and had a heart to serve women in ministry. The other woman was a dean for the Bible College. She spent extensive amounts of time mentoring young women. The third woman was me, and I was stunned. They called me forward, and I was given a basket full of lovely soaps, lotions, a bouquet of flowers, and a gift card to a salon. They honored me as a godly mother raising children for the Lord through a difficult situation. I sat and cried while surrounded by the gifts.

The silence from our church was based on an ignorance and so they did not know how to respond. It did not come from a heart that did not care. I had misjudged them (and others as well) because of their silence. The only reason I could comprehend the atrocities our family was facing was because I actually lived it; they did not. How many times had I ignored the pain of others out of ignorance or simply the fear of contracting their "leprosy?" My heart felt deeply encouraged and loved, even though at times it felt isolated.

Holly's dedication and my Mother's Day tribute helped me open up to the church again. I started to share what little I could with the prayer team and receive whatever support they could offer. I learned to share without the expectation that another person could carry what I was carrying. God had given me grace and strength, and it was why I still had my sanity. He had kept me as well. A sip of water when you are parched is not as good as a full glass, but it is better than nothing. I chose to open my heart and receive whatever support others could offer. It eased the thirst I felt inside.

CHAPTER 30 ✍

THE INTERVIEW

OVER TWO MONTHS had passed since I spoke with the DA. We were still waiting to hear if he would be pressing charges against my father on Holly's behalf. It had been more than a year since we had reported my father. The DA's office had been sent a second disclosure report, since the first one had been lost. For the next seven months, nothing further had been done on Holly's behalf. Now they even had a doctor's report.

I placed a call to the DA and was hoping to get an answer. However, it took a few days of calling before someone finally responded. The DA had the investigating officer return my call on his behalf. She informed me that the newly appointed DA had reviewed the recent doctor's report. He felt that it would be good if we brought Holly back into the Child Protection Services Investigation Center for another interview. They would videotape and record her disclosures. Any officers assigned to the case would listen and observe through a two-way mirror.

For the second interview, no questionnaire forms were required, and Holly was not undressed. After Holly's interview, I was taken back to the interview room with a two-way mirror and questioned. I told them about Holly's disclosures and answered questions regarding whether or not we had any contact with my parents. Then, I was asked about a man Holly had mentioned in the interview. She said the man was "Grandpa's friend" and wore a baseball cap and had an orange ponytail.

They asked if I had ever seen anyone who fit the description. I recalled a time when I was with my dad at a garage sale, and he greeted a man wearing a baseball cap who had an orange ponytail. He called him "Red." After we left the sale, I asked my Dad how he knew him. He said he had met the man in town and never gave me much more of an answer. There was something about the man that troubled me. He was rough, and I was surprised my dad knew him. He didn't seem like the type of person my parents associated with.

The CPS interviewer's eyes widened, "Did you know that there is a man that goes by the name of 'Red?' He wears a baseball cap, has long, orange hair, and was recently charged with sexual abuse and has disappeared."

"No, I didn't."

She changed subjects and informed me that Holly did well and reported extensively. She thought that what Holly had shared regarding her grandfather, his friends, and Naked Lady sounded like a pornography ring.

In response, I shared a memory involving my parents acquiring a storage unit from an auction that I helped them unpack and sort the items. Among the household junk were unlabeled VHS videos. Later that evening, after I left, my mom called and was concerned that I may have taken some of the videos home with me. She alerted me that the videos contained child pornography and she was going to take them to the police. I had not taken any, but I called the next day and asked what the police had done. She said she decided to just throw the videos away instead of going to the police.

The CPS interview concluded with their assurance that they would be sending all the information from Holly's evaluation to the district attorney. Once again, we waited and waited to hear back.

A week later, Ellen told me the investigator had called. She informed Ellen that they might attach Holly's case to Kristine's when they went to trial since Holly had "finally disclosed." The investigator further informed her that the recorder and the video camera "malfunctioned" during Holly's interview and nothing had been recorded. The officers on the case would just interpret what they thought Holly "meant" since they had watched through a two-way mirror. Then she asked Ellen a strange question, "Do you think it is possible for Holly's mom to have had time to coach Holly on what to say, since things have taken so long?"

I found it troubling that Ellen was called and I wasn't. CPS had not indicated any problems with the recording devices, but now the investigator said they hadn't worked. Once again, the investigator inferred a twisted view of the case. Earlier, she had implied my concern for other children being harmed was an attempt to strengthen Holly's case. Now the long delay was viewed as an opportunity for me to "coach" my daughter to lie. I was livid.

I repeatedly called the investigator, until she finally responded. She confirmed that the recorder and video camera had "malfunctioned," but she assured me that they could still evaluate Holly's disclosures without them. When I questioned her about asking Ellen if I had time to "coach Holly" on what to say, she denied it. I responded angrily, "Well someone is lying, either my sister-in-law or you."

She snapped back. "I am so offended. How can you say such a thing? This case is very near and dear to my heart! You know, I think we received a report, a complaint, yes, I believe we did, as I recall, a complaint was filed with CPS about your family."

"A complaint?"

"Yes, there was a complaint about the large number of children coming and going from your home." It was a veiled threat.

"Well, umm, we do have seven children." I redirected the conversation and questioned her about the doctor's report of physical evidence.

She responded that the DA wanted to query the doctor further as to whether something else could have caused the fissures, but the doctor had not returned any of the DA's calls. Then she ended the call by telling me all the possible options the DA may employ regarding Holly's case. However, she really didn't know what actions he would take or if he would do anything at all for that matter.

I called Doctor Gareth to understand why she had not returned the DA's calls. She told me she did not understand why she had not received any calls from the DA's office. After sending the report, she had anticipated some type of response from their office. She was willing to testify, if needed, but had not received any request or reply.

It was clear to me that the DA had all the necessary evidence for a trial, but it wasn't about evidence, justice, or protecting little children. It was about appearing as though they were going through the legal processes while having no intention of completing it.

In the end, the DA decided not to prosecute my father on Kristine's, or Diana's behalf. Kristine had been in my parents' care in an adjoining state prior to my parents' move closer to us. Abuse charges had been filed there as well. Since this state had decided to prosecute on Kristine's behalf, the DA decided to drop all charges, even though there were fewer charges filed in the other state.

He explained his reasons for dropping all the charges, "He is an old man; if we press all the charges, he could end up dying in jail."

The DA additionally refused to confiscate Dad's computer to screen for child pornography. Because Dad had initially turned himself in, Dad was able to plea bargain in either state. In the end, Dad spent six months in jail and exited as a registered sex offender with no press coverage. They still had not pressed any charges on Holly's behalf and did not attach her case to my niece's as well. Holly's case was just silently set aside.

I made an appointment with Fay to dump out the anger I felt over the injustice. She had been involved in social work for years and had frequently testified in sexual abuse cases. Apparently, this type of manipulation in a case meant one of two things.

She shook her head, "This isn't incompetence or budget issues. Someone has gotten to them, or there are people in the DA's office who are pedophiles and part of this thing themselves."

My father's jail time was like a slap on the wrist. He did time for such a short while that it would have been easy for my parents to cover up and maintain their deceptive front. They could tell extended family and friends that they were traveling in their RV for the past six months. They could improve their image by stating that they were busy helping Hurricane Katrina victims or use a thousand other lies, and no one would have known. Meanwhile, we had played "cat and mouse" with a legal system that was in my parents' camp.

We were in a small town where our four-year-old had revealed, in all likelihood, a pornography ring and snuff film industry with people that gave death threats, killed babies, and raped toddlers. By working through the legal process, being a caring citizen that abided by the law and followed legal procedure, it felt as if I had put Holly at greater risk.

Don't people need to turn in pedophiles to keep children safe? Isn't it important for a child who has been harmed to know who was the predator and who was the victim? Shouldn't the child know that something will be done about the "bad guy?" It felt like the legal system had lost all sense of who was the real criminal and who was the victim. While a child advocacy organization can help a child disclose and report for the purpose of prosecution, it is only beneficial if the criminal department does something in response to their reports. Now it felt like the wrong people knew how much Holly had remembered and exposed.

CHAPTER 31 ❧

THE PRESS

TRAVIS AND ELLEN were angry over the injustice that Dad had been sentenced to six months in jail in exchange for the repeated rape of Kristine and the sexual abuse and assault of Diana. The injustice was a mockery. In anger, Ellen anonymously called the newspaper press in the town where Wendell was the acting mayor. It was the same town where my parents had once served in various civic offices and were lucrative business owners, as well as the founders of the local bank.

The news hit half of the state newspapers and several Internet sites. The headlines read: "Former Councilman Guilty of Sexual Abuse," "Former Councilman Admits to Child Rape," and a few months later, "Sex Offender Former Councilman Released from State Prison."

The publicity made things awkward for Wendell. He was asked by the press to comment on the accusations against Dad and the sentencing and was quoted by newspapers throughout the state.

He said, "My father should not be judged by these questionable allegations but on his stellar record of service and upstanding character in this community. My father has demonstrated by his actions throughout his life that he is a moral, respectable, and a generous man. While the current situation is upsetting and painful for our entire family, I continue to be proud of my father, and I love him. I am confident that people who know him realize that there is much more to this story than meets the eye, but unfortunately, my father will not be able to reveal the full nature of this situation."

Wendell misquoted the charges and defended Dad further. "He copped a plea. He did not want to go into a court battle with the people who accused him of this. He was arrested on suspicion of eighteen sexual-assault-related charges. I think it says a lot when originally he was charged with twenty-six counts and they were all dropped except for two. The prosecutor lost faith in the case. The other indicator of his innocence is how the prosecutor recommended the minimum sentence allowable by law."

Wendell had never phoned Travis or me. His unspoken silence prior to the press release seemed to indicate where he would stand, but to act as though our father was the victim of false allegations was an even greater betrayal. In my grief, I wrote him a letter I never sent. I told him our parents were deceiving him and he shouldn't trust Mom and Dad. They shouldn't be around Wendell's newborn grandson. I told him I loved him, and then I tore up the letter. Wendell never heard me anyway. Since his divorce, he had changed. Whenever I talked with him, he made a practice of laughing at me, ignoring me, or trying to bait me into debates. It was ridiculous ... we were adults. I no longer played the game with him or chased him for more mistreatment, so he no longer wanted to interact. The letter was my way of releasing sorrow and giving Wendell to God.

After the call Travis initially made to Wendell, we never heard from Wendell again. I wasn't sure anymore of who Wendell really was. Wendell went on to open up several businesses with my parents and was listed as their only child on my mother's updated political profile.

A close friend, Elsie, who had been one of those who had prayed and anointed the prayer shawl from Vivian, read the news online. She sent me a long e-mail:

Dear Hannah,

I am just so sorry. To see full justice denied when such precious innocents have been so horrifically violated is beyond words! I want to *scream* out and tell the *real* story of this "good man"! Wendell was right about *one* thing: there certainly is more to this story! And to have Wendell defend him only adds to the devastation. What an understatement when he said the whole family is suffering over his father's situation! Does he think this was all made up? Or is he just protecting his *own* reputation by defending his father? A hundred and eighty days, a lousy hundred and eighty days, for abusing children! No, Wendell, the light sentence doesn't reflect your dad's innocence; rather it exposes the legal system's failure to protect children and punish those who hurt them! Hannah, your brother's words ring hollow in light of these charges. Your dad's reputation is forever destroyed. No matter how Wendell might want to gloss over this crime, people won't buy it. Rape of a child is a horrific crime, and any decent person reading the article will be equally horrified. We know that full justice will only be served before the Living God. Your father *will* have to answer to the Lord, sooner than he thinks. *Perfect* justice has already been served we just don't see it yet. Do we know that Wendell's children haven't been violated? I am just so sorry, Hannah—about *all* of it, of course. My heart has been so grieved over this unbelievable situation.

Then she wrote out a prayer:

Dear Lord, we stand with Hannah and her family, and we come before your Holy throne on their behalf. We know that nothing happens that you are not aware of, so we know that even the smallest injustice does not go unnoticed by you. You see everything and you know the hearts of the wicked. You know all the unspeakable ugliness that has come flooding into their household because of evil. Their battle (war!) will not be fought in vain because you are the Lord of lords and the King of kings who will bring justice at the perfect time. Lord, it is so difficult for us to understand why these things are allowed to happen, and why justice does not come when we so desperately desire it. Everything in us screams for justice! But we are so disappointed by this world's systems and by so many who are in authority—and even sometimes by those very people who claim to love us. We ultimately cannot trust in horses or chariots, can we, Lord? We continue to ask that *truth* would be revealed here on earth and particularly in this situation, that things hidden in the darkness would be exposed for all to see.

Father, I pray that you would put a hedge of protection around their home and around each member of the family. Jehovah Rapha, bring healing to their hearts, I pray. May your love and peace wash over them. Sustain them, Lord, especially Nick and Hannah. Give them wisdom and strength. Be the lifter of their heads. Show them great and mighty things, Father! And show them treasures in the darkness, Lord. May they remain always steadfast in you, abounding in hope. May their family continue to be a lighthouse in a very dark world. I pray your peace over their doorpost. May the Evil One have no victory over them at any time! They belong to *You,* Lord; they are *Yours,* set apart for you.

Thank you, Lord, for this family, and for the tremendous blessing they are to me and to others. We love them dearly, but not nearly as much as you do. Blessed be the Holy name of the Lord! Amen.

Elsie had come alongside me and was not afraid to see or hear my pain. Many times she would call and ask questions about our ongoing situation. I always felt the freedom to share, and she still asks.

I had grown up in the town where Wendell was now mayor. I lived there for eighteen years and attended the same church and school he had attended. Throughout my childhood, many people in the church had been like family. After the press release, I never heard from anyone. I assumed that if they were ever to ask my parents about Travis's and my well-being, my mother could easily make up some story. Perhaps she would say that Travis was after my father's money, and since they refused to give him any more, he was no longer speaking to them. She could easily say that Nick and I were part of some "charismatic cult" so they had broken off fellowship.

My parents were dispensational in their beliefs. The one time they had visited our church with us, they seethed through the whole service. Their personal views found the raising of hands and speaking in tongues during worship offensive.

If family friends questioned my parents about Dad's jail time, they could say that Travis had convinced me of false accusations against Dad, and I had taken up his offense. Regardless of what cover-up my parents could use, we would never hear from anyone in my hometown.

My uncles were also supportive of my father. "He is the most outstanding Christian man I have ever known," my uncle Archie replied when I told him about the situation.

At first, my Uncle Dwight seemed supportive of us. He would call to ask how we were doing and express how sorry he was. He even choked up on the phone when I told him that Holly had been harmed as well as Travis's daughters. Then he turned around and joined my parents on a cruise to Mexico.

I could not trust him, and I wondered if he was simply baiting me for information. I became more cautious when I spoke with him.

He invited me to my maternal grandfather's ninetieth birthday. My parents would be there, of course, since they lived next door to Grandpa and cared for him. My uncle felt that Grandpa should not suffer because of this rift in the family and that I should come for his sake. Uncle Dwight just didn't understand. I decided to write letters to both of my uncles, explaining that I no longer trusted anyone who socialized with the man who molested and tortured my daughter. I returned checks for Christmas gifts and told them that I would not be in contact with them any longer. Then I grieved because I had loved my uncles and had fond memories of them from when I was a child. Dwight continued to send Christmas cards, but I did not respond.

CHAPTER 32 ❧

ANOTHER GOOD-BYE

MY PATERNAL GRANDMOTHER, Dena, who lived near my parents, became another loss I would grieve. We would visit her often by stopping in after church to share a treat or to take her out for a Sunday meal. I had to explain to her about the abuse and why I could not bring the children over because she lived near my parents, who stopped in daily to check on her. At first, she was upset over the news and asked me what she should do. I set up an appointment for her to see a good counselor, and she went. We offered to relocate her near us, but she chose to stay near my dad. I understood that at her age and with my dad being in charge of her finances, such drastic changes felt too overwhelming.

For a short while, Nick would pick her up and bring her to our house for visits. When she would call, her chats would often center on my parents and the nice things they were doing for her, and that made it difficult for me.

Then one day, her tone changed, and in frustration, she left a message on our answering machine while I was away. "I wish you people would get things worked out with your father so that everything could go back to the way it was. In the Bible, wasn't David forgiven for what he had done? You just need to do the same with you father! I don't want you to pick me up after church this Sunday or for any more visits. I think it is best if I just stay put."

Grandma Dena continued to send the children Christmas money, but since my parents' names were on her checks, I could no longer accept them. I knew that I would have to let go of her, and it would be another loss without a funeral.

Months earlier, the Lord had given me an amazing dream to prepare me. I was in a house surrounded by green, grassy fields set in the Midwestern plains and was standing in front of a large window with Holly. My parents and Grandma Dena were in the room as well. I saw an approaching storm and stepped outside with Holly in my arms. On the horizon was a large tornado, and it was coming so fast that I had no time to seek shelter in the schoolhouse basement next door. I stood still and spoke to the tornado, telling it to lift and set down on the other side of the house, and it did. Then I returned to the house and warned my parents and grandma that the next time a tornado came, they should seek shelter in the schoolhouse basement. If they went to the basement, they would be saved. A woman with blonde hair and dark-rimmed glasses that I didn't recognize came into the room. She said she had the key to the basement, and then I left with Holly in my arms. In the dream, I understood that I would never see my parents or grandmother again, and I would not return to the house. I knew they had been warned about how to avoid destruction, and it was not my responsibility to protect them. I was supposed to leave them and protect Holly.

I wrote Grandma a letter, explaining the returned checks and that I accepted her decision to stay with my parents and no longer visit us. I affirmed my love and appreciation for her, but in reality, I told her good-bye.

CHAPTER 33

PSALM 10

PSALM 10 BECAME my cry for justice and my prayer to God. David penned my heart's anguish, so I used the words the Holy Spirit had given him. It was right to pour out my anger to God and to tell Him how I felt. It was right to desire that God defend us and uncover the evil that assaulted us. David knew that he could come to God with his anger over the injustices of evil inflicted by those that had mistreated him. He did not speak with sugar-coated, Christianized diction but was raw and honest before God. He put his confidence in a God who would one day bend down from heaven, with smoke coming from His nostrils and a devouring fire from His mouth, to vanquish the enemy (Psalm 18:8–9).

So I prayed Psalm 10:

Why do You stand afar off, O Lord? Why do You hide in times of trouble? The wicked in his pride persecutes the poor; let them be caught in the plots which they have devised.

For the wicked boasts of his heart's desire; he blesses the greedy and renounces the Lord. The wicked in his proud countenance does not seek God; God is in none of his thoughts.

His ways are always prospering; Your judgments are far above, out of his sight; as for all his enemies, he sneers at them. He has said in his heart, "I shall not be moved; I shall never be in adversity." His mouth is full of cursing and deceit and oppression; under his tongue is trouble and iniquity.

He sits in the lurking places of the villages; in the secret places he murders the innocent; his eyes are secretly fixed on the helpless. He lies in wait secretly, as a lion in his den; he lies in wait to catch the poor; he catches the poor when he draws him into his net. So he crouches, he lies low, that the helpless may fall by his strength. He has said in his heart, "God has forgotten; He hides His face, He will never see."

Arise, O Lord! O God, lift up Your hand! Do not forget the humble. Why do the wicked renounce God? He has said in his heart, "You will not require an account."

But You have seen, for You observe trouble and grief, to repay it by Your hand. The helpless commits' himself to You; You are the helper of the fatherless. Break the arm of the wicked and the evil man; seek out his wickedness until You find none.

The Lord is King forever and ever; the nations have perished out of His land. Lord, You have heard the desire of the humble; You will prepare their heart; You will cause Your ear to hear, to do justice to the fatherless and the oppressed, that the man of the earth may oppress no more.

I clung to the Psalms and held them close. I recited and proclaimed them until they became a continual dialogue of my heart that poured out in times of worship. Whole passages of Scripture resonated throughout my day. I was living, feeling, and devouring them as God breathed affirmation and courage into me with every word. Within them, He clearly defined the ways of the wicked and exposed evil.

Today's idolatry has been presented by the Western church as a lust for earthly pleasures, not as ancient, idolatrous pagan worship. That was the culture from thousands of years ago. The Scriptures did not appear as relevant in regards to the type of idolatry we were dealing with in Western culture today, at least not in literal form. Of course, it still applied on the foreign mission field, but we were more "civilized and progressive" in the states. Idolatry then was the same as now, and the church just didn't see it. Nothing had changed; it was just hidden.

Here in America, and in other refined countries, people gather secretively and dress in ancient attire to worship the same gods of Egypt by sacrificing humans and animals to gain power and favor. They perform the same sacrifices and perverse fertility rituals as those in ancient cultures. Then, following these rituals, they put on respectable attire and go about unnoticed. They will sit in church and smirk at those who warn of the idolatry of materialism, while the night before they washed their hands of the blood from infants offered to Moloch.

"God," I cried, "expose them, until you find none. Expose it all, everything my father and others like him have done. Let no evil remain hidden."

I cried out because I knew, as David did, that someday, He would.

CHAPTER 34   ❧

ATTORNEY

AFTER WITNESSING THE failure of the judicial system in the handling of our case, we knew a different avenue of "calling to account" was needed. This was not a slap-on-the-hand offence, and the justice system had been everything *but* just. We decided, at the suggestion of our neighbor Warren, to pursue legal action through the civil court. Warren told us that it had been his professional experience that the civil court system has better outcomes for victims of sexual abuse crimes. I began the search for a Personal Injury Attorney who specialized in sexual abuse cases.

The first one I talked with ended up being a bit strange. He had just won a large case on behalf of a man who had been molested as a child by a Catholic priest, so I figured he'd be competent. His phone interview focused mainly on questioning me to determine if I was ever harmed by my father, rather than the details of Holly's harm. I repeatedly told him I had no memory of any harm and was in shock over my father's behavior, but he continued to press the matter. He asked if I had ever been treated special, like a little princess. When I began to retreat from this strange form of questioning, he changed direction and decided to consider taking on our case and scheduled an appointment with us. He wanted all of Holly's disclosures, drawings, and the videotape of her playing married.

His office was affluent. The conference room had rich leather chairs and a long mahogany table. He spoke compassionately about our plight and then hurriedly glanced through Holly's drawings. The rest of the time, he summarized his own personal experiences of abuse and the amnesic barriers that had surrounded his memory. With his scattered approach, Nick and I realized that if he charged by the hour and did most of the talking, we would receive little from a settlement after paying the hourly fees. He asked to keep copies of Holly's work and her video for review while we took a few days to decide about retaining him.

We chose not to continue and asked if we could pick up the video. He was unavailable when we endeavored to recover it and after several attempts, I gave up. Why he wanted to keep the video was a mystery to me, but it caused me to wonder how safe it was to enter into another legal system in the same region of my parents' residence. I prayed, "Lord, direct me. Help me not waste time looking for the wrong attorneys or end up at the wrong place."

In a random search, I came across the Internet site for the attorney Neil Morgan, whose specialty was sexual abuse cases. His site expressed compassionate concern for victims with a link to an orphanage that his firm cosponsored for sexually-abused girls who had been imprisoned in the sex trade in Africa.

Mr. Morgan was curt and brief on the phone, and I felt like I had to spit things out quickly. He was not charming or compassionate, but a tough attorney which was what we were going to need. He agreed to meet with us to consider taking our case.

During our meeting, he asked numerous questions and then made a phone call to the DA with us in his office. He politely explained to the DA that he was considering taking on our daughter's case as a personal injury civil case. He wanted to understand how the DA stood regarding bringing charges against my father on Holly's behalf and where they were in that process, since no action had been taken. Was this still something they were considering? After several answers of "yes" and "I see," he thanked the DA and hung up.

Staring intensely at me, he asked pointedly, "Are there any doubts at all about what your daughter is telling you, any doubts as to whether it is true?"

I blurted out. "I wish!" The tears pooled in my eyes as I fought to hold back the anguish.

"Good. Okay then, here is what you need to do. The DA doesn't believe your daughter. He thinks this is 'fanciful,' so I need you to do two things."

He scrawled out on paper in large capital letters.

"VALIDATE" and "VERIFY."

"How can the DA say this is fanciful after her exam and disclosures? How can he say that?" I was so angry at the deceitfulness of the DA's statement.

"It doesn't matter. He can, and he is indemnified, which means you can't take him to court or press any charges against him, so there is little you can do about it. Rarely does anyone take on a county. I certainly wouldn't, not on this. We can still file a civil suit, we have the fact that your father has served time for this type of behavior in our favor, but I need for you to validate what she has told you. Get her to someone qualified—a doctor and counselor with a PhD—someone who can get on a witness stand with good qualifications."

"We have already begun that, she is seeing Dr. Vera Miller."

"Good, go regularly, and also write up a time line as best you can of when she was in your parents' care, when she started disclosing, and anything you noticed. Then get it to me. I also want you to get your brother here. If we combine cases, it will be much stronger."

I tried to warn him about my brother being very unstable and a challenge to work with.

"Well, maybe you will be able to get him some money, which may help. I will take this case, but he must be on board."

Softening his tone he asked. "What church do you go to?"

"We go to Metro Bible Church," I answered.

He smiled. "I do too; I thought I had seen you folks before."

Nick chuckled. "Yeah, with a family of nine, we are hard to miss."

Then he told us how sorry he was about what we were going through. He shared how he and his wife had opened homes in Africa for girls who had been abused. The place I had read about on his website was a partnership he had sponsored with our church. Afterwards, he closed with prayer for us. Nick and I knew we had come to the right place and that God had led us. He had gone before us and lined up good help. Though Neil's tone earlier had been gruff, we discovered he was also tender and caring. The job required a tough exterior, but it was the opposite of what was in his heart.

Getting Travis to see Neil was not the easiest endeavor. Travis was suspicious of everything and everyone, but he was more desperate for money. He was three months behind on his electric bill, and Mom had now withdrawn all of her financial support. The county offered him only food stamps and a limited amount of counseling, but counseling was cut off due to Travis's inconsistency in keeping appointments. Without the counseling, he could not renew or refill his prescriptions for antidepressants.

I did my best to convince Travis of the benefits of a civil case versus the injustices we had suffered in the judicial system. He knew that we were trying to do the right thing regardless of how difficult it was. He also realized we had put up with his angry outburst, blunders with our parents, and emotional instability. Finally, after weeks of cancelled appointments, he met with Neil.

It was a long meeting. Travis asked about a hundred questions, needed everything extensively explained, insisted that Neil reword trite phrases in the standard retainer documents, demanded Neil reduce his cut on the settlement, and requested lengthy coffee breaks in order to reconsider before he finally signed. I was amazed at how well Neil handled Travis.

Later when my brother left the office, Neil took me aside. "Boy, your brother is a piece of work."

"Now you understand why I was uneasy about him being a part of this case."

Neil nodded his head in agreement, and I doubted Neil would want Travis on the witness stand.

CHAPTER 35 ❧

MEMORIES

JUST AS THE first attorney questioned me if my father had harmed me, other people questioned as well. It seemed to be the number-one question I was asked by anyone that knew of Holly's situation. Sometimes it angered me and made me want to snap back, "Do you think that if I had memories of sick things happening to me, I would have left her with him?"

I was tired of being scrutinized, but the question started to eat at me. I shared my struggle with Fay during a counseling session.

"Is it possible for nothing to have happened to me as a child, even though my father had this secret dual life? I am so tired of people asking me over and over if anything happened to me, like it is expected!"

"Yes, I believe it is possible, probably very rare, but entirely possible. I have never encountered it, but that doesn't mean it isn't possible."

"Well then, do you think I could have lost memories and have amnesic barriers? Do you think I could have MPD?"

"Hannah, amnesia has a wide scale. It ranges from highway amnesia (driver's daze) to full-blown MPD on the other end of the scale. I do not think you are on the far end of that scale. I do, however, think there is a possibility you could be somewhere on the disassociated scale, but not at the far end. Why don't we look at what you know and remember and go from there and see what God shows us. Would you be willing to do that?"

"Yes."

"Okay, have you ever had a reoccurring dream?"

"Yes, it isn't always the same in the details, but there is always the bad feeling. I'm always on this desolate road on white hills, lost or stuck, with nowhere to go and no way to get out. Sometimes the white is snow, but mostly it is small, white gravel in a desolate desert setting. I hate the dream, and always feel horrible when I wake up."

"Should we ask Jesus about this?"

"Yes." I nodded.

She began to pray, "True Lord Jesus, could you reveal to Hannah the source of this dream?" Nothing happened.

"It just feels dark and quiet."

Her tone changed. "In the name of Jesus, I bind every Antichrist spirit that is seeking to interfere with this prayer time. I also bind any spirits that would seek to deceive, in the name of Jesus."

"How will I know it is Jesus showing me something and not me making it up?"

"Well, do you normally make things up?"

"No, but how will you know that the enemy isn't just deceiving me?"

"Didn't we just bind him according to Scripture? As children of the Lord, we have authority to do this, and whatever we bind on earth is bound in heaven."

I relaxed and softened my heart in prayer, trusting that the Lord would lead me as He had in my prayer times with Holly.

"Just close your eyes and let me know if you sense or hear anything from the Lord." Fay then prayed quietly to herself for me.

The next thing I knew, I saw the white gravel roads in my mind. I was small, about two to three years old and was standing on the road. I started to feel uneasy. "I feel afraid."

"Are you able to continue and trust Jesus to help you?" Her question redirected me away from the fear and helped me focus on the One who was in charge. I felt more peace.

"Yes, I can continue."

"Okay, try to see what is around you in this place that Jesus is revealing." Fay began to pray, "Lord Jesus, could you bring more revelation as to what this is about?"

I saw to the right of where I was standing what looked like my mom in her early twenties. She was lying on the ground, her head was by a rock, and blood was trickling from the corner of her mouth. I had this awareness that she had quarreled with my dad, and he had hurt her. I told Fay what I was seeing.

"Can you stay present with what you are sensing and seeing?"

"I can."

The next thing I saw was my father putting my mother in the back seat of a white station wagon and closing the door. Then he drove off and left me standing in the white gravel desert. I stared at the sky and focused on the clouds like I was no longer on the ground, but as if I were a cloud too. Suddenly, I felt arms lift me up and hold me. I was no longer only sensing and seeing in our prayer time, but I was literally feeling. While I could still feel the couch I was sitting on, I also felt physical arms around me. I felt a soft, wool beard graze my right check and smooth flannel of a linen robe. The robe smelled like the fresh air after cooling mountain rains—sweet, but even better. I began to cry.

Even though I was sitting in her office, I was also taken to another place, and it was no longer a memory being recalled. The arms of Jesus felt more real than the couch I was sitting on. My sense of smell, touch, and sight all beheld Him. I could barely speak or move. Fay asked me what was happening.

"Jesus is holding me. I just want to stay here."

"You can stay."

I finished my session in His arms. The experience was real, and I did not feel the slightest question about its validity. I also did not question the validity of the memory, because Jesus does not comfort deceptions. I had never experienced Him in this way. The realization that I had an amnesic memory was not as overwhelming because I had just experienced how He could change the bitter to sweet. I knew that only He knew what was broken off from me. Although I connected with the sadness of having been so small and abandoned for an unknown period of time, the bad event was now a treasure. I know what Jesus smells like, the touch of His beard, and the feel of his robe. I also knew there was no way I could have willed the memory into consciousness because it was lost to me. If I had been able to recall any of this on my own, I would have. The trauma I had experienced at such a young age had shattered it from my awareness, and all I had were confusing, reoccurring dreams.

When I went home that evening, I searched online for desert areas that were within driving distance from the area where my father worked when I was two to three years of age. He had to travel due to a shortage of local employment. I found images of a remote desert area that had long, winding roads on the crest of white gravel hills in the same area he had been employed. In looking through photographs from my childhood, I found the station wagon I saw in my memory.

I continued to see Fay until her practice relocated near her grown children, who lived out of state. Only a few isolated memories different from Holly's were ever revealed in my counseling sessions with Fay. The desert memory was the most clear and intact. I could only conclude that perhaps my father's sick skill at harm was in its early stages when I was young, but it increased over the years. Now Travis's dysfunctional behavior began to make me wonder if Dad's skills were acquired at Travis's expense.

CHAPTER 36 ❧

PRAYER

ENTERING INTO THE legal arena made me feel vulnerable again, and combining our case with Travis's felt even scarier. We needed more prayer support from people we knew would not gossip. Nick suggested I call our Bible study group leader and ask him if he thought our group would be willing to uphold us in prayer as we went through the civil court proceedings. Our leader, Chad, agreed to allow us to present our situation to the group, but to do so in a way that only gave away the most basic details of our situation. He was concerned it might be too hard on some members of the group, and less information would protect confidentialities we needed to keep. We were the youngest couple in our home group with ages running from forty-four to ninety-three. All the members were seasoned prayer warriors.

As I shared with them that Holly and my nieces had been abused and that we were in civil case proceedings, Ed abruptly got up and left the room. God had used Ed in Holly's healing. She loved the small home group filled with safe grandmas and grandpas, and Ed was her favorite. At one of the home meetings, she walked over to him and he reached down to set her in his lap. My stomach tightened as I watched his every move and wondered if Holly would trigger.

At that time, Ed and the others did not know about Holly's abuse. Her response was a miracle. She looked up at Ed's face and laid her head against his chest. She sat there for a long time, and Ed's hands remained still as he leaned his head over hers. He was so gentle, as though he sensed her fragility. He had no idea how God had used him to heal our little girl. She found a grandpa that wasn't a scarie, and from then on, Ed was no longer just "Ed" to Holly, but "Papa Ed." When he suddenly left the room, I was concerned.

Chad was concerned as well and went to check on Ed. Chad found him crying outside, unable to handle the news that someone had harmed Holly. He cherished her like a granddaughter and loved our family as though we were part of his own.

Ed, his wife Darlene, as well as others in the group prayed for us faithfully. Darlene would often call for updates and would pray for me over the phone. Throughout the whole civil process, it was obvious we were covered by their prayers. The information we chose not to share did not limit the directing of the Holy Spirit in these precious saints.

CHAPTER 37 ❧

SETTLEMENT

IT TOOK OVER a year before our case settled. Neil had to hire a forensic financial investigator, since my parents would not cooperate and give him the requested information. When Neil showed me the report, I told him I knew there was more and gave him whatever I could remember. My parents had corporations, associations, investments, as well as their own financial trusts. Some of their assets were discovered and some were not. Some were "gifted" to my brother Wendell or tied up in business partnerships with him and others. With a conviction on my father's record, it was in his best interest to settle.

The settlement was far from what we had requested, but our attorney felt it reasonable in comparison to other cases of a similar venue. It also kept Travis off the witness stand. What was left of the settlement following the court, filing, investigator, and attorney fees was put into a trust for the girls. Yearly, we would be required to report the use of their money to the state. The money was only to be used for the girls' recovery until they turned eighteen. Within the first year, Travis and Ellen began to use their daughters' trust fund for a variety of things—some for the girls and some to pay bills. They intended to pay back the trust. I just cringed.

CHAPTER 38 ❧

ANOTHER LOSS

TRAVIS WAS BORN when I was ten. When he was a baby, I couldn't stand to hear him cry, so I would sneak in his room and rescue him from his crib. Mom would scold me and tell me I was spoiling him, but I kept him with me and watched him, so she usually let it go. When he was two, I would babysit him while my mother worked at my dad's office. At age three, he would ask to sleep with me when he was scared and snuggled next to me. Later in high school, I became involved in extracurricular activities after school, and before long, I was off to college, so I saw less of Travis. In his middle teens, Travis went through a rebellious phase. He started running away, getting involved with the wrong crowd, and married young with a pregnant bride.

Following the settlement, Travis began changing from being broken and dysfunctional to seething with anger and grasping for a sense of power in exchange for years of feeling helpless. However, the power he pursued was dark. He started volunteering at a haunted house in the mall and spent hours working on sets, costumes, and make up. He took trips to learn more on staging horror. He would tell Ellen that when he dressed in costumes for horror shows, he felt as though something would come over him and change him into the character he portrayed. It was unsettling to him, but he continued all the same by giving more of himself to it. He even included his children in some of the performances, having his eldest son Bronson depict Satan Junior in a "father and son" show. The shows were intended for comedy, but they were more offensive and foul than funny. I couldn't understand how he could take his children to these shows when some of them were suffering from the same abuse as Holly.

In spite of their limited income, Travis invested money in a professional filming camera. He planned to generate additional earnings to supplement his part-time job by filming various "gigs." He filmed performances for the haunted house that would be featured as an advertisement online. He also filmed showgirls and exotic dancers from strip clubs. He would promote them while advertising his film industry. Ellen would call upset, but that was the extent of it. The fight seemed to have gone out of her as she twisted and rationalized his behavior until it became acceptable. Travis's eyes became cold and hard as an unseen wall closed around his heart.

Several months after the settlement, Ellen called asking for money. Their electricity was being shut off and they needed to pay a fee to keep it on. I suggested to her that Travis sell his expensive camera and stop spending time at the bars. Ellen agreed with the idea, but she didn't think he would listen. I told her I would need to talk with Nick first about giving them money. We had just given Ellen $200 a month earlier so she could renew her beautician license, and now there was a need for more.

That same evening, Travis called. He had not spoken with us for months and wanted to know if Nick had made a decision. Nick had just come home an hour before with a notice that his job status was uncertain. The company was downsizing, and he wouldn't know if he would be laid off until after March. Nick felt that if Travis indicated a willingness to turn his heart to the Lord and stop participating in ungodly activities, we would help him, even if money was tight. Travis was not interested in changing; he just wanted money. If we helped him now, we would be enabling him to sin and to survive without seeing his desperate need for God. Nick denied Travis the money, and Travis cursed.

"You are dead to us," Travis said and then slammed down the phone. Travis's value of our relationship had become purely monetary. This was the last time we talked to him.

The next day, I tried to call Ellen, but she wouldn't pick up. I left messages, but she never called back. Close to Christmas, I left a bag of gifts for the children and a card on their doorstep while they were gone, but I never heard back. I grieved the loss of being able to check from time to time on how the children were. I had tried to be a lifeline to them.

I would catch glimpses of their current activities on public blog profiles. Kristine posted original poems and writings about feeling broken and not remembering her childhood. They were heartrending and full of the pain of a young girl who needed help. Travis's blog continued to feature him with scantily clothed women and in grotesque getups. He looked weighed down, depressed, half-dead, and much older than I. What had happened to the brother who used to end his phone calls with, "Love you, Sis"?

CHAPTER 39 ❧

MYSTERY AND
A BAPTISMAL

DIRECTLY ON THE heels of losing Travis, Jed and Lydia called. They were home on furlough from overseas missions and wondered if they could stop by to visit on their way to speak at supporting churches. They had been encouraging to us through prayers and counseling in e-mails, and Lydia would call when she felt burdened and offered her listening heart. They knew some of the horrible things we had been facing, and it was wonderful to see them. Jed enjoyed playing with the smaller children while Lydia and I talked and laughed about the kind of grandpa he would make. We sipped coffee while sitting on the deck as we quickly caught up in the limited time we had together.

When things quieted down with the children, Jed and Lydia asked how we were doing. They understood the effects of trauma and the need to share what happened as a part of the recovery process. In their ministry, they had counseled many tsunami victims and displaced war refugees. Before they left our house, Jed gently spoke to me about my parents. "I think you will always live with a level of mystery."

He knew I was still trying to make sense of what had happened to Holly and who my parents really were. His words went deep into my heart, and I knew he was right. What God withholds belongs with Him. Jed spoke like a compassionate brother, and even though I lost two earthly brothers, I knew I had this one for eternity. We said our good-byes, not knowing when we would see each other again. Now that the company Nick worked for was officially closing, we didn't know if we would be relocating from the area they visited on furlough.

In spite of our financial uncertainty, we were seeing the miraculous recovery of our little girl daily. Periodically, throughout the past two years, I continued to stay in touch with Colette from Ellel. She suggested that we baptize Holly as part of her healing. She had used the Anglican Baptismal as a guide for baptisms, and it was meaningful for those to whom they ministered healing at their center. Earlier in Holly's recovery, she triggered from taking baths and was fearful in water. I had to stay continually by her side. She disclosed having been pushed under water and held down by my father. The bath she had taken earlier with the oil had brought her peace. Being in water had changed from being a bad experience to being somewhere Jesus met her and brought healing.

We talked with her about being baptized. She had seen Ann baptized at church in front of three hundred people, and at first, she was uneasy. We explained how it would be only her family watching and she would be wearing her swimsuit. We would use the garden tub, just as we had for her special, anointed bath; she liked the idea and seemed excited.

When the planned day arrived, Holly and Nick wore their swimsuits, while the rest of us put on nice clothes. The bathroom was cozy, with all of us gathered around, and the atmosphere was full of worship. We walked through the Anglican Baptismal prayer booklet together, and then Nick gently guided Holly forward in the water (which felt safer to Holly). She rose up out of the water, her face aglow with joy. She wrapped her arms around his neck while he held her and prayed. We all choked back tears and applauded. To help her remember this special day, I gave her a pretty doll dressed in a white gown I had purchased online. Our third-eldest son, Jeremy, took pictures as well, and then we went downstairs to have a celebration meal together. I had a deep sense of overcoming. Today had been a day of washing off ashes and adorning a garment of joy.

Holly began sleeping in her room again. She knew if she had a bad dream or became scared, she could always come back to our room. We switched Holly and Ann's room with one of her brother's and repainted. She had a new bed, bedspread, dresser, and now a new room. It felt lighthearted, and from the window she could see her friend Abby's house, so Holly knew when Abby was outside and could play. My heart lifted and filled with hope as I watched the healing taking place. Even her sand-tray sessions with Vera were changing. Less ominous figurines were placed in the tray and the "worlds" she would make were increasing in beauty.

Then one morning she awoke with a big smile. "Mommy, guess what happened last night!"

"What?"

"I woke up scared, like a scary was going to pull me away from you, and when I opened my eyes, I saw a big, big angel!" Her arms reached high over her head to emphasize his massive size.

"He was right above me and his face was right in front of mine and he was really bright! He smiled at me and said, 'Don't be afraid.' I fell right asleep, Mommy. I wasn't scared!"

From then on, her nights were more peaceful, and nightmares became the non-norm.

CHAPTER 40 ❧

MORE HARM

A CHANGE WAS coming soon. Nick had sent out his resume to different companies, and responses were coming in. I knew I needed to prepare for the likelihood of a move. I asked the older children to begin cleaning out their dresser drawers to get rid of outgrown clothing or gifts from their grandparents that were missed in my earlier purge.

That afternoon, I found Jeremy slumped over his top dresser drawer, crying, with a pile of sorted clothes on the floor.

"Mom, I loved this tie. I used to wear it when I was little. I felt like a big man when I wore it. Grandpa gave it to me. It was great-grandpa's."

"I know honey. I am so sorry. You will need to get rid of it, though."

I put my arm on his shoulder. In my research, I had read about some of the evil rituals that are practiced with men donning red bowties and dark suits rather than robes.

"Jeremy, because it came from Grandpa, we needed to get rid of it. We don't know what it may be connected to. I have read that people involved in what he was have bowtie parties, where sick things are done."

Suddenly Jeremy turned to me, pale, with a horrified expression. "Mom, I know about the bowtie parties! Mom, how do I know? How do I know?"

My stomach tightened, but outwardly, I remained calm. "Why don't we ask Jesus how you know about these parties?"

He sat down next to me on his bed, and I began to pray, asking the Lord to show Jeremy how he knew about this.

"Quick, Mom! Quick, get me a piece of paper!"

Jeremy, artistically gifted and very perceptive, quickly sketched in great detail a room similar to pictures I had seen of Masonic temples with red curtains and high-back padded chairs. In the middle was what appeared to be a small altar. Tears filled his eyes. "Mom, I remember!" Deep, groaning sobs shook him, and he collapsed over on the bed. "I remember."

When he was able to speak, he continued, "Grandpa took me here when I was small, like two or three. He wanted to put a hidden mark on me, like an "S" or "J." He was using some kind of hot ointment that burned. I pulled my hand away and wouldn't do what he wanted. Mom, he was mad, really mad! He took me out into the alley and took my pants off. He laughed at me and hit me in the head. He said I was stupid … he said I was stupid!"

Jeremy looked at me, stunned, with tears running down his face. It was only the first of a handful of memories that would be uncovered in the next three years. I could count on one hand the number of times he had stayed with my parents at that age—on one hand! When Jeremy was a baby, we lived on the West Coast. Once a year for Christmas, we flew out from the West Coast to visit my parents on the East Coast. Since our wedding anniversary was close to Christmas, my parents would gift us with a belated anniversary night alone. They paid for a nice dinner and hotel room, offering to keep the children for the night. The two times they had offered this gift, Jeremy had been two and three years old.

There was never anything to indicate that Jeremy had been harmed; however, he acted excited and clingy when we returned. This seemed normal to me, since I never left him overnight. He appeared to love his grandpa as a young child, and he loved working in the shop with him as he got older. At age four, he began to have reoccurring night terrors, and it was difficult to wake him. He also had difficulties learning all throughout school and struggled in learning to read. Now thirteen years later, he suddenly triggered from a bowtie connected to the word *party*.

What slowly unfolded were memories of four to five isolated events on the same horrible level as what Holly had endured. For years we thought his learning challenges were related to a time when he became critically ill as a newborn and was hospitalized. We had him tested numerous times to understand why he struggled. The results all showed learning disabilities related to language processing with no genetic or physiological cause. Now I began to wonder if the learning delays and struggles had been the cause of inflicted trauma. He was harmed at a crucial age for language and processing development, which are foundational milestones prior to reading.

Jeremy began to walk through a valley of anger and grief over the aspects that were torn from his childhood. This valley of horrible images not only involved my dad but also my mom molesting him. He finally made sense of the bad dreams and flashbacks he felt too ashamed to share but was secretly tormented by for years.

Two years later, we sent Jeremy to Ellel for a training and healing retreat. He came back different. As God washed away the horrible images that tormented Jeremy, God gave him heavenly pictures to capture the Lord's healing in amazing drawings and paintings. The boy who struggled with words and felt insecure when expressing his heart with others was anointed to speak a language with art that went beyond vocabulary and in every dialect.

Now I had a mounting concern for our youngest son, Timothy. My dad hurt boys too. Holly had mentioned seeing Timothy poked like she had been, but Timothy denied the event. I had not known what to think about what she shared. Every time we questioned Timothy about being harmed, he assured us that nothing happened. I did not question the validity of what Holly said, but for Timothy to have no memory of being poked, he would have to be shattered. For Holly to have seen him being poked, he would have been six years old at the time.

Fragmentation would have happened when he was younger, before the age of five. The original trauma that fragmented him would have caused a younger part of his personality to identify with abuse and remain in an amnesic state. Any further abuse would trigger him into the same state and be isolated from his six-year-old awareness. He could have gone through the abusive event with Holly and have no conscious memory.

The only time I ever left Timothy with my parents prior to the age of five was when we moved back to the East Coast. Nick had taken a job north of where my parents lived and had to start right away. My parents offered to help with the little ones while I stayed to finish the packing. I followed with the moving van and our large dog across the states to our new home. Nick flew out with the younger children and left them with my parents for five days, while he began his new job a few hours away.

Mom took pictures of all the fun things they had done with the children, and when I would call to check in, she went on about how they were enjoying their company. She even made a scrapbook of their time together as a keepsake. Timothy was two years old at the time. After we were settled, my parents relocated closer to us.

I now saw the twisted, sick pattern of how my father targeted that age group. He moved quickly and skillfully in evil, with my mother's assistance, attempting to fragment their memories in short periods of time so all would appear normal and the children would never say a thing.

CHAPTER 41 ❧

GOD SEES

I ONCE AGAIN felt the flood of anger, rage, anguish, and numbing shock. This evil deception had gone on for years. The secondary post-traumatic stress I felt as I walked through the horror of Holly's disclosures and the dam of emotions from the past two years began to feel it would burst. Even though I had processed a lot in counseling with Fay regarding Holly, every new exposure of harm brought another level of grief.

Fay now lived out of state, as she had moved to be closer to her grandchildren. She had referred me earlier to a licensed therapist, Charla, as a consultant on spiritual warfare for Holly. I decided to set up an appointment and begin to counsel with her.

My sessions with Charla felt like walking into a lovely, peaceful garden. It felt safe enough for a person to face anything and still feel the love of God and His acceptance. I would enter her office burdened and leave wrapped in peace. She encouraged me to begin setting aside time to grieve over my losses where I could be alone and just cry. With the awareness that Jeremy (and possibly Timothy) had been harmed, the grief intensified. I was afraid that if I began to grieve, I would fall apart. In a time of prayer with Charla, the Lord assured me that if I faced the pain and grieved, I would not lose my sanity. In letting go of control, I would heal. After all, He is the one that holds our sanity in His hands. Still, setting aside time to grieve was a bit challenging in a household of nine, and I was protective of Holly seeing me upset.

The strain on Nick and me was huge. People we had trusted and loved had taken advantage of our trust and had violated what was most dear to us. There was no place to put this in our understanding. Nick grew tired of all our conversations being so weighty, and some days he just wanted to fix things and not have to listen about what was broken. On one of those particular days, he was fixated on repairing his computer when I came in wanting to talk. I had felt so bad about all that he was carrying, as though being my parents' daughter made it my fault. The reality of being unloved and even hated by my parents had caused me to ache for reassurance that Nick loved me unconditionally. I knew he loved me before this storm had hit, but did he still love me now? Out of pain I had asked, "Given what you know now, would you still have married me?" He was angry; how could I even think of such a question? Hadn't he proven it over and over again in his commitment to me!

"What does that matter, it is what it is." He snapped and turned back to his computer.

That did it. The dam of pain burst. In a huff, I grabbed some toiletries and stuffed them in my purse. I decided I was leaving for the night, and I would let him know how much he had hurt me. He wasn't seeing my need for his affirmation. Instead, he had just made me feel that he would not have married me if he could go back in time.

That was more than my heart could take. I stormed downstairs and grabbed the car keys just as the phone rang. Nick answered. It was Jed, and he had something he needed to tell me. I glared at Nick as he tried to hand me the phone, and I stormed out the front door. I was not about to talk to anyone! I heard Nick mutter something to Jed about it being a bad time as I shut the door. Nick did not know that I was leaving for the night. He thought I had gone to the store.

I drove north for two hours and then turned into a dumpy motel. We did not have the money for a nice motel, and the dumpy motel seemed to reflect how I felt. In anguish, I yelled at God in route, "Do you even see me? Do You?"

How would I go on? I had no place to go and no one to run to. How could I go on being married to a man who felt stuck with me? How could I still function at home, acting as if all was well with the children? My chest hurt, and it was hard to breathe. I had never felt pain so deep, even after all I had been through with Holly. This was a flood of pain I was unsure I would survive. I had never cried and wailed like this. Years of sorrow, a lifetime it seemed, was crushing my heart. I did not feel God's comfort. I felt alone, and God seemed so far away.

I berated myself. I was so full of self-anger. I had stormed out the door, with no thought as to how it may have impacted Holly. I raged inside for being so self-absorbed and deserting my precious little Holly. Was she once again feeling fear and abandonment, not knowing where I had gone? What kind of mother was I? Two, and in all likelihood, three of my children had been abused by my father and mother, and I never saw it. My poor husband was stuck with a mess. Who could blame him for not wanting me? With the torment inside, the torment around me, and the lies of the tormenter, I was a wreck.

Later in the evening, I called home and Joseph answered, "Mom, are you okay? We are missing you. What happened?"

I didn't want to say much to him, "I'm not okay, but I will be. I'll be home tomorrow. I'm at a motel. I just needed some time to think. Can I talk to Dad?"

"He's busy making supper. Do you want me to have him call you back?"

"Yes," and I gave Joseph the motel number. "Is Holly okay, and is everyone else doing all right?"

"Yea, Mom, we're all fine, just a little worried about you. I'll let Dad know you called."

I waited a long time for Nick to call, and the longer it was quiet, the more I felt it confirmed my deepest dread. He was stuck with me and would not have married me given the chance to do it over. Even so, somewhere hidden deep inside me something held on to a belief and hope that I was wrong. I had to be; I just couldn't handle it being any other way. As it grew late, I started wondering if Joseph maybe forgot to give Nick the number, so I called again.

Nick answered the phone. "Yes, I got the number and the message."

"Then why didn't you call?" I burst out in tears.

"Honey, do you want to tell me what this is all about? I didn't call because it has taken me awhile to put some worried kids to bed. They are okay, but I had to spend time reassuring them."

I cried even harder. "Are they okay? Do I need to come home now?"

He gently responded, "They are okay. I just told them you needed a break and that sometimes moms need to get away. I told them you'd be back tomorrow. They were a little upset, but they are fine now."

Then I told him that I didn't know how I was going to function as his wife. I would go on and do my best to cover up what I felt. It just hurt so bad to think that he didn't want me, but I understood. As I sobbed, I told him that somehow we would have to make it work for the children's sake.

When my tears subsided, he spoke, "Honey, I have never not wanted you. I was just angry at your question. I committed myself to you for better or worse. I am not happy about what has happened, but I still love you."

There were apologies back and forth and a realization that we needed time to heal with each other. We needed to learn to laugh again and have time away as a couple. Surviving this was different from thriving. We needed to learn to thrive and to find a way to rebuild joy in our lives as we came through this carnage. He told me to get some rest and come home in the morning, when I felt ready. I wanted to pack up and leave then, but it was after 11 P.M. As long as it was safe for me to stay, he felt it would be better if I rested.

Before we hung up, he mentioned Jed's earlier call. "Oh, by the way, do you want to hear why Jed called?"

"Sure." I answered half-heartedly, feeling guilty for how I had responded earlier.

"He said God told him to call you and give you a message. He told him to tell you, 'He sees you.'"

This time, the tears were of overwhelming gratitude. I was angry, but before the pain in my heart had even formed the words, God sent an answer just for me. It reads in Isaiah 65:24, "It shall come to pass that before they call, I will answer; and while they are still speaking, I will hear." He had done this just for me. The God of heaven had come down when I could not hear Him over the roar of the storm inside and around me. He brought me a message I so desperately needed. *He sees me.*

CHAPTER 42 ❧

EXTENDED FAMILY

NICK WOULD BE taking a new job in a different area, and we would need to relocate. Before we moved, I wanted Holly to meet what little extended family I still had who believed what had happened. They saw in the papers the news about my dad and Wendell's comments on the matter. I had called my cousin, Deborah, four months prior to the press release. We were invited to a family reunion they were hosting, but we could not go since my parents and uncles might attend. When I explained why we could not come, she was shocked and enraged, then told my great-aunt. Auntie tore up and burned the letters my mother had given her, and she no longer communicated with her.

We were moving far away from them and would not have an opportunity to see them again for a while. So Holly and I took a train to visit my great-aunt and my cousins down south.

I asked Auntie why she believed me, since she had been like a second mother to my mom when she was growing up. Auntie slapped the table, used a colorful expression, and retorted, "Kids don't make this stuff up." I told her only a small portion of what had happened to Holly, and it was enough.

Holly loved being around them and for me, it was a sense of a childhood I could retain. It was family that had been authentic in my youth and loved me, not simply because I was related to "outstanding

Christian" parents. When they realized how my uncles had responded to my father's abuse of Holly and my nieces, my aunt and cousins became guarded in their conversations with my uncles. They also withdrew from those in the family who interacted with my parents.

My cousin, Callie, had worked with the police department for years and knew about pedophiles and sexual abuse. She worked on some horrible cases during her employment, and was angered by the phony Christian exterior she saw in my parents. Feeling betrayed by them as well, she sent them a scathing letter to break all contact with them. She offered to be supportive of us as much as needed.

Holly and I returned home with fond memories of late-night talks, laughter, good food, shopping, and tender moments. Deborah's husband, Joel, was caring and sensitive with Holly, and she felt safe with all of them. Auntie tucked a few tatted doilies in tissue paper for me to keep as heirlooms that I could pass on to Holly as a reminder of our special time. We cried when we parted from them, but also left with a sense of joy and relief. I had not lost all of my relatives to my parents' deception.

CHAPTER 43 ❧

RECOVERY

HOLLY HAD GONE through so much in the past year and a half. The more she disclosed, the more she rolled on the waves of post-traumatic emotions. Adrenaline fueled her reactions to everything when the circumstances did not merit the intensity of her responses. Dr. Vera had sent us to a neurodevelopment center that specialized in RAD (Reactive Attachment Disorder) typically seen in children that have been abused when very young or have experienced some type of trauma in infancy. Sets of exercises were prescribed daily to retrain the brain to calm itself and release less adrenaline. We walked her through these exercises for six months and coupled them with Play Therapy, trampoline jumping, rockie time, drawing, and most of all prayer. We had watched her transform from days where emotional outbursts were her main form of expression to days replaced with emotional calmness and her rediscovery of little-girl play.

Our second eldest son, Peter, helped her with the exercises and had a knack for making her laugh. He would plop on the floor next to her and play sock puppets or act out the silliest of stories with her little dolls. She loved every minute of it, and to hear her giggle and laugh again was a joy. Oh, how we had missed her laughter. Peter, a human teddy bear, was part of her return to joy, and God used him to teach Holly how to play again. It comforted him to help her. He had tried to contain the anger and pain over what happened to her, but it weighed on him. I would happen upon him brushing away tears in attempts to be strong, as though in doing so he could lift some of the burden off of us.

The weight lifted when he played the piano, and our house filled with God's presence as hope built again. His gifted ability in composing worship music drew Holly in like a magnet. He would set Holly on his lap, teaching her notes and little tunes. This was the beginning of her love for music, and then she began to sing. We were amazed at her beautiful voice. Now at only five and a half years old, she sang as though she had taken voice lessons and had been schooled in music. God had given the little girl who was silenced by abuse a beautiful voice full of anointing and tender worship.

Holly was more stable now, and we hoped our imminent move would be less unsettling for her. My biggest concern was her having to leave Dr. Vera. In anticipation, Dr. Vera began preparing Holly for the changes and for saying good-bye. They both made a beautiful memory book where Holly put the pictures she had drawn during her sessions. Vera added photos she had taken of Holly and her sand-tray worlds. She and Vera wrote about how Holly felt when she first came to Dr. Vera, how she felt now, and the healing that had taken place. The book depicted the incredible journey Holly made and the people who made it with her. Holly would always be able to see the healing journey God brought her through and her miraculous recovery. God gave man free will, which allowed her grandparents to choose evil and hurt Holly. God immediately lined up all the help Holly would need to heal and recover. In the end, she would walk away with more treasure and faith than the pain she had experienced.

Whenever man makes a destructive choice, God already has a restoration plan in place for both victim and offender through his Son Jesus and those that love Him. Her scrapbook would remind her of this truth. Vera told Holly that no matter where we moved, Holly could always call her if she needed to. She also affirmed Holly in the strength God had given her and the support she had with her family. Vera then spent time preparing me for a season where we would be without a qualified counselor for Holly.

"I think that Holly will be all right without a qualified counselor for now. She has plateaued and is in more of a resting state with all that has happened. She has made amazing and miraculous progress. At crucial developmental phases and changes in her life you may find her struggling and in need of more therapy. You will have to walk through this again with her at each of these times. As a child grows, they process trauma through different levels of maturity. When she begins puberty in her teen years and interacts with boys, during college, and if she marries, these will all be times where she could revisit what has happened and need help and support through the process. She has done well, but it is still a journey of healing, and there is a long road ahead."

On the way home from our good-bye session, Holly cried a little and then fell asleep. The past year and a half had been so hard, and I wanted to see healing, then move on and put this behind us. I quietly poured out my heart to the Lord.

"God, will my whole life be restoration?"

Before the thought ever escaped my lips in a quiet cry, God answered me, *"Mine was."*

It caught my breath at the suddenness and depth of His reply. The words He spoke held volumes, and a holy hush filled my heart.

"Yes Lord, it was."

Jesus had given everything; His very life was for the restoration of His children. His followers were also called to be restorers. It was part of being a disciple. It was a bended knee, a Lordship, an open hand, and a moment where I recognized Jesus as the author of my destiny, not me. I had embraced this journey, and it had changed me.

CHAPTER 44 ❧

FRAGMENTED

WHILE HOLLY WAS stabilizing, Timothy increasingly struggled. It was becoming obvious that he had been harmed even though he still had no recall. He was clever, and it had been easy to teach him to read, write, and launch him into school. Now he took hours to complete small amounts of school work, and I would find him staring off into space. As impending change with Nick's job loomed on the horizon, Timothy became progressively worse. Change seemed to scare him, and his unusual behaviors intensified.

He was obsessed about being poisoned. Every chemical was a hazard and every germ was lethal. He got hand soap on his lip; would he be okay? He bumped the baby on the head; would she be okay? The disinfectant he used on the toilet might be on his skin; what should he do? The obsession with poison intensified to the point that even brushing his teeth became a major ordeal. He was convinced that a drop of toothpaste would injure him. He would also repeatedly wash his hands until they became raw and bled. I had to limit his hand washing to restroom use only and monitor him since he would try to sneak more washes. Holly once shared that Timothy was forced to poke her, hurt a baby, and take yucky pictures with her.

One morning while I was caring for Phoebe, Holly had come into my room and plopped on the bed.

"Mom, I poked Timothy. Will I go to jail?"

"No, little girls don't go to jail. They don't put little girls in jail."

Timothy never spoke of any of these things and denied Holly ever poked him. As his behavior worsened, we decided to take Timothy to a child therapist. The appointments were costly, and our insurance did not cover them. Timothy enjoyed the sessions since they involved "play," but minimal real therapy took place. Timothy was just there to play and was resistant to discussing anything more in depth.

Timothy became increasingly edgy with Holly, often lashing out for no apparent reason or glaring at her with an uncanny detest. When corrected for being spitefully mean, he would play innocent or blatantly lie, even when we had just witnessed the behavior. It didn't matter if we witnessed him hit or shove her, he still would twist the story and attempt to reinterpret it for us. We would ground him, make him clean the bathroom, and do push-ups or sit-ups when he was defiant. Holly would yell at him when he mistreated her and tell him he was acting like Grandpa. This seemed to stun him and make him withdraw.

One evening after being grounded for his behavior towards Holly, he went into the bathroom to take a shower and slammed the glass shower door in anger. The glass shattered, and Nick had to carry him out of the shower to avoid the bits of glass all over the floor. It had become apparent that Holly was a constant trigger to something he couldn't remember.

After we moved, Timothy began to feel safer, and the intensity of the obsessional behaviors lessened. Knowing that Grandpa did not know where we were initiated a release of memories. I began to take him to another counselor. It was a four-hour drive to Dr. Avery's, who was the most qualified counselor I knew of in the state. We learned with Holly that a level of skill was required to help a child recover from ritual abuse, and it is difficult to find counselors that are qualified.

Timothy now shared memories similar to what Holly shared but the process was much slower. He had fragmented, and Holly had not, so the damage was more difficult to treat. The five days he spent with my parents when we moved from the West Coast had given my dad plenty of opportunity to shatter him at the preferred age of two.

Jeremy was almost seven when they stayed at my parents' house, so I questioned him to see if he remembered anything happening to Timothy during their stay. He recalled how my parents would take Timothy into the back bedroom and told Jeremy they needed to "spank him" because he wouldn't take his nap. Jeremy would hear Timothy cry and he felt helpless, unable to protect his brother. When Timothy came out of the room, he had an empty, vacant stare and wouldn't speak. It was the silence and distant look in Timothy's eyes that Jeremy found upsetting.

Jeremy also recalled my dad taking Timothy away on three separate occasions for the whole day. He asked if he could come along, but each time he was told "no." He remembered feeling afraid as he watched my dad drive off with Timothy. When they came back at night, Timothy would not talk for the whole evening and most of the next day. As Jeremy shared, he began to weep. Timothy had been hurt as he had been, and Jeremy had been unable to keep Timothy safe. He had not known what Grandpa had done to Timothy on their outings.

Once again I thought of Job. I felt surrounded by ashes and broken pottery that cut into festering pain. Three of my babies! They had hurt three of my babies, and my soft, gentle, little Timothy was left shattered. Had he wondered why we left him? What had they said when they hurt him? Did he wonder where I was? Did he wonder if I was ever coming back?

I now recalled that he began needing a nightlight in his room after staying with them. Then he started having nightmares and developed a stutter between the ages of four and five. Like before, this was one of those 20/20 hindsight moments which now made sense.

When he was small, I checked on him at night while he slept and would lay my hand on him to pray, "Make this one a preacher, Lord."

Now, he was in a battle to possess a faith that had been sorely tried before it had a chance to grow. With the body of a thirteen-year-old and the feelings of a traumatized toddler, he seemed lost in a storm of conflicting emotions.

At one of Timothy's counseling appointments, Dr. Avery sent Timothy to the waiting room and asked me to come into his office. With his eyes full of tears, he questioned, "How are you doing?"

He was stunned at what Timothy recalled during the session and at what our family had endured.

"If you ever need to talk, please feel free to let me know. I would be more than willing to be supportive."

I thanked him.

Then shaking his head, he commented, "Your father ... wow, what an evil man. He should be in jail for life!"

"Yes, I know. Someday he will answer to a higher court."

CHAPTER 45 ❧

SCATTERING ASHES

THE MORE I understood God to be a God of justice, the more I could release my need for it. I knew I needed to stay on the path of releasing ongoing forgiveness and leaving vengeance to God. I did not want to give Satan a foothold. I wanted nothing to do with the enemy's camp. I could not judge my father's heart and become imprisoned in the quagmire of bitterness.

I did not know what happened to twist and corrupt my father, only God did. Was he tormented with fears for his life? Was he extremely fragmented as a child? Was he made to believe he was dark and evil? Had he found himself so entrenched in a secret society or high levels of evil that he believed he could not escape? Did that despair lead him to surrender his soul in hopes that his obedience would spare others? Had he become one that promoted, embraced, and completely sold himself over to evil? Was evil what he loved? Had he entrapped my mom, or was she a part of some masquerade?

I wondered what had changed her many years ago. Why was she so concerned about her aging face but not about her weight? She would repeatedly have plastic surgery for minor changes, and yet her aging appearance remained the same. It was all a mystery. Sometimes I wondered if she was really my mom, or if she was just someone made to resemble her. It appeared irrational to think this way, but she seemed so disconnected and superficial. I rarely felt that I was speaking to the "real" mom I knew when very young.

For whatever reason, my parents were entrenched in the sickest of evil. If they repented, they would have to confront the horror of all they had done. Facing it would be a hell on earth, so to speak, but a hell on earth is better than hell for eternity. If they repented, they would become completely different people than they had been. They would be new creations transformed through the blood of the true Lord Jesus. His blood holds more power than any ritual man has ever performed. They would be washed and made righteous. True salvation always causes true change. They would be given a desire to be holy, a longing to be closer to Him, and a passion to be like the one who had saved them.

Psalm 16:4 reads, "Their sorrows shall be multiplied who hasten after another god; their drink offerings of blood I will not offer, nor take up their names on my lips."

For two years, God would not permit me to pray for them, and then one day I was released. My prayer was that my father would end his days as Manasseh. Manasseh (2 Chronicles 33:1–20 and 2 Kings 21:1–18), built up altars and high places to many false gods and to the stars. He sacrificed his children in the fire and was said to have filled Jerusalem with innocent blood. God warned Manasseh of coming destruction if he did not turn from evil, but he did not listen. Manasseh was taken by hooks and fetters into captivity in Babylon by the king of Assyria. While in captivity, he greatly humbled himself before God and was permitted to return to Jerusalem where he spent his remaining days. There was hope for Manasseh, and there is hope for those who partake in the darkest of evil. Jesus' power to forgive and deliver us is bigger than any sin and mightier than any devil.

On the cross, Jesus paid for what my parents had done. Every drop of his shed blood is priceless, and to refuse His payment is to trample and belittle His costly sacrifice. No matter how angry I felt toward my parents and their "friends," I must forgive them. Forgiveness is not reconciliation and can be given without ever seeing the offender again. Withholding forgiveness cheapens the price Jesus paid on their behalf. It is a statement that says more payment is required. In praying as Jesus did while on the cross, "Father forgive them, for they do not know what they do" (Luke 23:34), I released them into the flow of His forgiveness and His judgment. My parents and those they partnered with must choose either to humble themselves as Manasseh by stepping into the flow of forgiveness, or refuse and remain in the flow of judgment to receive the outpouring of wrath. However, that is between them and God.

Jesus delivered us from the kingdom of darkness. Do we realize how dark that kingdom is or how deeply it twists its prisoners? He does. He suffered everything that man has, endured every sin, and was tormented by every demon in hell. His death on the cross was not merely physical, but there He entered a realm of suffering that no human could endure. When babies are murdered, it is done to Him. When children are raped, it is done to Him. He chose to identify with our pain and suffering to deliver us from the kingdom whose goal is our destruction.

Our family has had a closer view of the intense darkness of that kingdom, and I am more grateful to have been rescued from it. The demonic deceptions and twisting caused by that kingdom leads to a reprobate mind. It becomes a mind that is debased and seemingly inhuman. Seeing the darkness has made us hunger for more of the light. It has sharpened our awareness of how important it is for us to err on the side of holiness. One does not err when they embrace more of holiness (being set apart to the Lord); they err and erode when they don't.

Manasseh also had a grandson named Josiah, and at a young age, he chose to follow the Lord. He purged Jerusalem of altars and ritual booths. He defiled the places where children were sacrificed to Moloch and removed the idolatrous priests and those who burned incense to Baal as well as other false gods. He burned images, ground them into ashes, and threw them on graves. He burned the chariots that were dedicated to the sun, broke down and pulverized altars which the kings of Judah and his grandfather made. In the place of the sacred pillars and wooden images, he put dead men's bones. He crushed and burned the high place at Bethel. Then he took the bones out of the tombs that were there and burned them. Long story short, Josiah spread ashes throughout the whole country. The land had become increasingly cursed by the sins of those that lived in it. The ashes showed an abhorrence of those sins, and sorrowful repentance because of them (2 Kings 23:4–21).

I felt stirred by what Josiah had done. I took the remaining letters and cards from my mother and father that I had missed in the earlier purge. I burned them. I spread the ashes along the river where my parents had lived when they harmed Holly. I took ashes to the house where we lived when I was a child and spread them at the entrance to the property. Then I scattered them at the Christian school my father helped build and the church I had attended as a child. I wept over the sins of my father and mother and asked God to cleanse the land. Land has history. I wanted history to write that although evil occurred on the land, repentance for that evil had taken place as well.

CHAPTER 46 ❧

NEW VIEW

THROUGH THIS JOURNEY, my discernment has changed. I no longer consider the black attire of a teenager as more indicative of evil involvement than a man I sense darkness upon who is wearing a uniform or suit. I do not regard some holidays, like Halloween, as an opportunity for evangelistic community outreach. Rather, I recognize it as a pagan holiday that is observed as a high satanic, holy day involving perverse rituals and human sacrifices. Therefore, I will have no part of it in any form.

Instead, our family chooses to celebrate the Feast of Booths (Tabernacles). It is the holiday God gave us for the fall and focuses on God's coming to earth to "tabernacle" (dwell) with us. We pitch a camping tent and decorate it with flowers and garlands. A Nativity set is placed on a table inside the tent, and we read about the true Lord Jesus who came to dwell with us.

I question why some churches give preference to harvest parties that are mixed with Halloween beliefs when they could be celebrating God's holiday of Tabernacles. Christ partook of this celebration while on earth (John 7) and we will be celebrating it with Him when He returns. In fact, those nations that do not partake of this celebration will receive a plague and have drought (Zechariah 14:16–20).

We also avoid the Ishtar fertility traditions so often mixed with what is known as Easter. Instead, we have a Passover Seder on Resurrection Sunday in memory of the night Jesus was beaten and taken to the cross. We teach our children that the Passover lamb was a picture of Jesus, the Lamb of God, who was given for our sin. We remember how God delivered His people from captivity in Egypt and how He delivers us through His son.

I am protective about what I permit my children to set before their eyes. Their eyes are the windows to their soul. I keep them away from cartoons and movies that blatantly or subtilely exposes children to witchcraft. I look for the roots in things and teach my older children to do the same. If the root is evil, it will not be growing in my home.

The Bible says we will know if a tree is good or bad by its fruit (Matthew 7:16–20). If the root is evil, so is the tree and fruit, but few believe this. People partake of the fruit thinking it is harmless by joining exercise classes, organizations, societies, and using alternative medicines. They have no clue as to what their activities are rooted in or the history. Some will decorate their homes and attire with popular symbols and foreign figures, while unaware of the demonic idolatry they represent. I used to embrace and promote practices simply because they were taught or offered by a "good" Christian. The fact that it is endorsed by a Christian does not make it spiritually acceptable.

I look at men with Masonic jewelry, hats, and bumper stickers differently as well. I refuse to visit their various lodges or lodge-sponsored events. I do not attended Shriner (33rd-degree Masons) hosted circuses or events, seek their medical services, or donate to any Masonic temples or affiliated clubs. I do not attend churches where the pastor or church leaders are lodge members, nor do I promote their covering of light by supporting their ministries.

While I understand that some lower-level members of these societies believe they are simply helping others and are perhaps unaware of what evil they have joined, those at higher levels understand and are aware of the evil teachings of these societies. The oaths taken in their secret meetings are pledged to the pagan deities of Babylon, and the morning star they revere is later revealed as Lucifer. It is not uncommon for some high-level participants to join with high-level satanic priests in the ritual abuse of children. They pervert justice and deceive the public by working together to gain political and spiritual power, and will protect each other from exposure. They put on "darkness for light and light for darkness; … bitter for sweet and sweet for bitter" (Isa. 5:20).

I was now cognizant of the fact that the grandfather I cherished, who helped so often at church, and was buried in a Masonic apron with a litany of accolades attributed to his high-level Masonic involvement, lived a deception of dualism. After his funeral, I found a Masonic book in his bookcase titled *Morals and Dogma of the Ancient and Accepted Scottish Rite of Freemasonry.* It contained sick perversions of ritual worship to pagan deities. The deception my grandfather had lived now flourished in his son. God had revealed that my father was deeply involved in dark druidic and Masonic practices.

Holly and Jeremy had drawn many pictures of or identified costumes, Masonic temples, regalia, ritual scenes, occult as well as Masonic symbols, swords, knives, druid staffs, and ceremonial hats. The children's pictures matched many of the Internet sites that boasted these evil practices. The abuse they disclosed echoed with similarity to hundreds of survivor voices on blogs and chat sites who congregated together to be heard, because society wasn't listening. While my father had an impressive bio in Christendom, he killed babies, bowed to gods formed from rocks and bones, and chanted to invoke evil spirits. The God I serve is stronger than his false gods, and my God had lifted my father's skirts and uncovered his nakedness. He had shown me things I never fathomed my father could partake of or embrace. In Luke 8:17, it reads, "Nothing is secret that will not be revealed," and in God's time, it all will be uncovered. Evil will not be able to continue to wear a covering of light, and it is only a matter of time.

The Word of God, the spiritual war manual full of accounts of those who encountered and confronted evil pagan nations, is now even more alive to me. The early church's Bible was the Old Testament. Today in some churches, people glide over these accounts and think they apply more to ancient times. Yet, that decadent culture the church came out of in the past is also a part of the present culture. "That which has been is what will be" (Eccl. 1:9). However, now evil hides, smug and deceptive, in dry churches where pastors or members wonder why their church is dying. They do not recognize the demons that slip in with members who are dualistically serving evil while appearing as devout Christians. Some serve what appear to be benign levels of compromise with evil while going through religious motions, others more fully in secret worship of Lucifer. In Ezekiel 23:39 it reads: "For after they had slain their children for their idols, on the same day they came into My sanctuary to profane it; and indeed thus they have done in the midst of My house."

Now I could see the truth, so I prayed, "God make me a female Elijah and Elisha, with the faith of a Shunammite woman. God, make my children Daniels, Josiahs, Deborahs, and the Elishas and Elijahs of today. And when You return, find faith here in these children and in those to come after them, if You tarry."

CHAPTER 47 ❧

HIDDEN HARM

TWO YEARS AFTER we moved with Nick's new job, we celebrated the marriage of our eldest son, Joseph. The wedding was breathtaking and full of worship. We danced to praise music, and God was greatly honored. Then three months later, I received a heartbreaking call from my daughter-in-law, Daisy. Joseph was not doing well and had been falling apart since they returned from their honeymoon. He was having what appeared to be horrific flashbacks. For a moment, he would act like a panicked child, and in the next, he would be in a rage before collapsing in tears. It was then that we found out he had been triggered through the intimacy of marriage by memories of perverted, sexual abuse and trauma that had shattered him around the age of two or three.

Joseph had honored God and remained pure. He had even waited to kiss Daisy until he proposed to her. They had done everything right and wanted their marriage bed blessed and honorable before the Lord. There had been nothing to trigger Joseph or to surface hidden memories. Like Jeremy, I could count on one hand the number of times he had been left with my parents at the age of two.

When Joseph was two, I had been on bed rest for six months with preterm labor while pregnant with his brother Peter. I was on several doses of medication and was monitored daily. The most I could do was crawl to the bathroom or take a three- to five-minute shower. The rest of the time, I lay in bed with pillows propped around me. Many friends from church came over and helped with Joseph, and there were two weekends my parents offered to pick him up and keep him—the weekend I went into labor and the weekend Nick had flown out of state to his brother's wedding.

Joseph was a very busy little go-getter from day one and was even more challenging as a teen due to his strong leadership tendencies. At times, he struggled to stay focused in school, but there had been no hint of anything amiss with him and my parents. Now, our lovely son, full of gifts and abilities, shook and choked up when he spoke and wondered how he would go through the process of recovery in the midst of a new job and a suffering marriage.

Changes of all kinds overwhelmed him as though a lack of consistency made him feel lost at sea. He would call Nick daily just to hear his father's voice and know that somewhere in the world, things were the same. Nick now became Joseph's source of support as I had been with Holly. However, Joseph was a grown man trying to deal with reoccurring emotions of a two year old, hold down a job, and not scare his wife.

We had recently learned about an intensive prayer and counseling ministry called CARES, that worked one-on-one with the survivors of ritual harm helping them recover from shattering. Nick longed to be a mirror of the Father heart of God to Joseph. He wanted to help Joseph by reassuring him of God's unconditional love for him, and more importantly, by being a conduit to re-connect Joseph to his true healer.

"Don't worry, Son, a father's call is to restore. I will cover your expenses."

Nick pulled the five thousand dollars out of our savings in faith. I booked the airline tickets and hotel before sending the deposit to reserve Joseph's ministry time. Nick and Joseph spent five intense days at the ministry center. When Joseph returned, he was equipped with the tools to help him cope. He had worked through some rough ritual memories, but was still very broken and struggling in his marriage.

Once again, I sank under the waves and depths of grief. Once again, I cried out, "God, *four* of my children! *Four*! So much precious time has been stolen from me. Instead of them knowing my love as toddlers, they knew the lies of abandonment, and it kept a part of their heart isolated from my love for so long! God, I want to hold them again. I want to hold that part of their history, that part of their hearts, and rescue them from harm, and be there to see their pain and take it away. I want to hold them as babies again, but the time is past and I can't! I can't hold the part that was locked away inside of them, so far from my love, and it hurts so bad, so very bad!"

"I know, I know how that feels." His voice echoed back at me, and once again I felt a hush.

"Yes, You do, Lord. You know how this feels, and You feel its pain every day. How many of Your children believe when something bad happens that You have abandoned them and just left them? I have. How many of the lies of the enemy keep me from knowing Your love and not allowing You into my pain? And it hurts You, like this hurts me. I see God, I see. I feel the longing, I feel the ache. Help me not believe the lies. I don't want lies to keep me from Your loving heart and Your longing arms. Hold me Lord, hold me."

One Sunday, a messianic Rabbi came to our church as a guest speaker. Feeling prompted by the Lord in the middle of his message, he pointed into the audience and declared, "You have received programming in your mind from the enemy's lies. God is bringing wholeness and removing the enemy's lies, and it is happening now. Be made whole in Jesus' name."

Joseph instantly felt a tingly surge go through his whole body, and when he left the service, he left changed. It was a profound miracle. A sense of stability and capacity filled Joseph. An internal shift towards wholeness began to pull him together. What takes years to overcome, sometimes a whole lifetime, began to rapidly occur inside of Joseph. Daisy saw an immediate change in his stability and emotions.

Joseph would still have a journey of healing ahead, but now he had the stability to address the pain. His wife had also been harmed by a family member as a child, and now the two of them would be recovering together by leaning on the Lord to carry them through. Like Nehemiah, they would be rebuilding walls to hedge out the enemy while wielding the sword.

Joseph would go forward to cast visions and spearhead ideas that would propel people into new territory. He would do so knowing that God was his foundation and never changed. He could face the risk of changes and new visions on the sure footing of a faithful God. I would prayerfully be alongside them, watching to see God perform miracles in their marriage. Joseph and Daisy would have amazing encounters with the Lord throughout their journey and would become curators of a catalogue with incredible healing testimonies. As they saw how God would bring them through any storm, it empowered them to confront the demonic waiting on any shore.

CHAPTER 48 ❧

GOD MOMENTS

FOR OUR ANNIVERSARY, Nick and I returned to the beach. We stayed in a different town than when this whole journey had unfolded five years earlier. As we were walking along the sandy shore, I silently prayed, "Lord, it would be nice to find a sand dollar that is whole, but I never do. They are always broken from the rough surf."

I no sooner completed my prayer, when my eyes landed on a very small sand dollar. It was the size of my thumbnail and completely whole. As I picked it up, God spoke to me, *"See, I can bring small, fragile things through rough waters whole."*

Now, it sits in my china cabinet as another treasured keepsake, just like the Garfield Band-Aid box.

Then one Sunday morning, God spoke to me at church during worship. My thoughts were wrapped up in the song and He unexpectedly turned my focus, catching me by surprise. *"When you felt Me hold you in the desert and you thought I was healing your memory, it wasn't Me entering into your memory, it was Me releasing your memory and bringing your past forward into your awareness."*

I thought He revealed a bad memory that broke away due to trauma and was making the bitter sweet in doing so. The truth was that He had physically been there, and had actually picked me up and kept me. Where was God when I was abandoned? He was there holding me, and I just hadn't been aware.

"You connected to Me then, and I kept you; that's why you recognized My love in Ivan."

Ivan was an older man in the church where I grew up. His eyes shined and oozed the love of Jesus; he called me his girl and gave me the safest, warmest hugs a little girl could ever receive. I used to think that Ivan was why I understood Jesus differently than my earthly father did. It was because of Ivan I begged to go to church, and it was Ivan who came and got me when my parents couldn't attend. However, he was not the reason I first connected to Jesus. Jesus himself snatched me out of the kingdom of darkness in the middle of a desert at the age of two and then told Ivan to love me as He does.

Another Sunday during worship, I suddenly became aware of an amazing peace covering me. With closed eyes, I saw what looked like a huge, velvety soft, white feathered wing. Covering me, it arched above my head, but still felt roomy under the wing like a downy cave.

"Remember the bubble you prayed around Holly?"

"Yes, Lord."

"This is what it was." I stood there in awe. How much do I not see, but it is still there just the same?

While standing during worship one Friday evening at a revival meeting, He suddenly spoke to me so strongly that I had to grab my seat because the weight of His presence and voice had made my legs go weak.

"Judas betrayed Me, and I knew it. I knew he would, and I let it happen for the glory it would bring. Your father betrayed you and your children, and

I knew it. I knew he would, and I let it happen for the glory it will bring. I am the one responsible, not you."

I slumped over in my chair and wept. The weight of shame and self-condemnation was gone, and it felt as if I had dropped the pottery shard I continually used to scrape the pain. The ashes on my feet had been washed away and replaced by the oil of the King. The King of kings passed by me as He did for Israel and saw me naked and struggling in blood as He had seen them. He covered me in embroidered cloth, soft shoes, and silk.

"Dance with Me, dance with Me," He invited.

CHAPTER 49 ❧

IN CONCLUSION

GOD'S ASSURANCE AND faithfulness has given me a confidence that our family will continue to heal and God will use us. We have come through a funnel, and our shape has changed. We are different than before, but still going through the process. Lies of abandonment and mistrust continue to be uprooted during amazing moments in God's presence. What our family has endured is no longer as overwhelming as it was at first. I have seen that God is bigger than what we have faced. We "stuck with Him," and that has made all the difference. There is no other option or path than His and no other way to overcome and heal. His way is the only way to true life. Any other path winds back to a kingdom of destruction. All that we have gone through will be for His glory. In faith, Nick and I believe and declare our children will "rebuild the old ruins, they shall raise up the former desolations, and they shall repair the ruined cities, the desolations of many generations. Strangers shall stand and feed [their] flocks, and the sons of the foreigner shall be [their] plowmen and [their] vinedressers. But [they] shall be named the priests of the Lord, [men] shall call [them] the servants of our God. [They] shall eat the riches of the Gentiles, and in their glory [they] shall boast. Instead of [their] shame [they] shall have double honor and instead of confusion they shall rejoice in their portion. Therefore in their land they shall possess double; Everlasting joy shall be theirs" (Isa. 61:4–7). For out of the ashes we rise!

In Conclusion

A Daunting Experience
(A poem written during the time I learned of Joseph's harm.)

It was a daunting experience
A horrific event
It was beyond scope or reason
But He didn't relent

The sovereign met with the why
The anguish with the appearance of a closed eye

The timing horribly wrong
How can this happen to me?
The footmen trampled the chariots so strong
Ran over again and again,
Where was the Savior, Redeemer, and Friend?

Healing and the miraculous I could claim,
The possibility I could see
But this was the lion raging, tearing
And God didn't show me
And I didn't ask,
Why would I? It was hidden and black
My father devoured in deception
While I only loved him back.

My heart was ripped
The treasure plundered,
My precious child torn from me
In the night, while I lie asleep.
In the day my father would smile, give a kiss on the cheek
Then secretly rape and plunder
In an evil grossly deep.

Duplicity masks the face of depravity,
It ravished the man that cared for me.
Hidden deep within
Behind a façade that to many
Was the epitome of well-bred men who preach of God.

Out of the Ashes

His seed had a role in being my earthly dad
He serves the gods of Nimrod, Manasseh, and Ahab
I chose to serve the God of the living, not of the dead
The God of Elijah has fathered me instead
To believe more in the power of the dark
Is to succumb to a weakened philosophy.
To defeat it
Is to believe in its future destiny.
Overcoming faith is not forged in a God you can see
But in the God of Abraham—as you chose to believe.

My knee is bent under His course for me
And I realized the lie of self-made dreams

His Lordship has given me
A passion for His glory,
Living out a divine destiny
Where time stands still, and hell and heaven see
That though the lion tore, I will still believe.

WinePressPublishing
Great Books, Defined.

To order additional copies of this book call:
1-877-421-READ (7323)
or please visit our website at
www.WinePressbooks.com

If you enjoyed this quality custom-published book,
drop by our website for more books and information.

www.winepresspublishing.com
"Your partner in custom publishing."

CPSIA information can be obtained at www.ICGtesting.com
Printed in the USA
LVOW102017091012

302146LV00013B/11/P

9 781414 122953